YANKEE STADIUM

Also by Joseph Durso

CASEY: THE LIFE AND LEGEND OF CHARLES DILLON STENGEL
THE DAYS OF MR. MCGRAW
AMAZING: THE MIRACLE OF THE METS
THE ALL-AMERICAN DOLLAR: THE BIG BUSINESS OF SPORTS

YANKEE STADIUM

Fifty Years of Drama

JOSEPH DURSO

Illustrated with Photographs

1972 HOUGHTON MIFFLIN COMPANY BOSTON

TO MY FATHER

"He shows you stars you never saw before."
— Shakespeare

ILLUSTRATIONS

"The Yankees will have to build a park in Queens or some other out-of-the-way place. Let them go away and wither on the vine."

John J. McGraw, 1921

"The cheers which greeted Babe Ruth when he stepped to the plate could be heard throughout the land."

— The New York Times, 1922,
reporting on the first radio
broadcast of the World Series

"This is the way old Casey Stengel ran running his home run home when two were out in the ninth inning and the score was tied, and the ball still bounding inside the Yankee yard."

— Damon Runyon, 1923

The Battle of Broadway, 1923: John J. McGraw versus
Babe Ruth.

The Yankees arrive with famous friends, too, like Lord and Lady Mountbatten, who lend aid and comfort to Colonel Jacob Ruppert as his baseball team assaults the entrenched Giants.

of the eighteen nineties, and as a result of both experiences was sensationally equipped for life in the nineteen hundreds.

He was five and a half feet tall with straight hair parted left of center above a square face and an immovable look. He had his shirts and shoes made in Havana, where he replenished his spirits by winter for the struggles of summer, and he had such short arms that he needed to have his suits tailored to fit. And when he arrived in New York in 1902 as the manager of the Giants, he wore high starched collars, four-in-hand ties and a fleur-de-lis pin embedded grandly in the center.

Against the cold of New York's winter, he would

bury himself in a fur-collared greatcoat and beaver hat and would look more immovable than ever. "His very walk across the field in a hostile town," observed Grantland Rice, "was a challenge to the multitude." To Gene Fowler, he was "stoutly knit, as game as a pit-bird, and very much in earnest when socking time was declared." And to his wife, Mary Blanche Sindall of Baltimore, he was — with affectionate understatement — "a young man of indestructible confidence."

Part of his indestructible confidence grew from the fact that McGraw had grown up as the runt of the litter in baseball leagues manned by roughnecks. Before he was twenty, he was contriving something called "inside baseball," a form of strategic piracy perfected

3

The Yankees, in fact, have come a long way from the time when they performed as the Highlanders at 168th Street and Broadway . . .

by the Baltimore Orioles in the days when they most nearly resembled the Lavender Hill Mob in full flight.

They played before clamorous crowds in a city that was known, in tribute to its passionate past, as Mob Town, and they played it with tricks like the hit-and-run, the drag bunt, and the Baltimore chop — with such muscular enthusiasm that John Montgomery Ward, the manager of the New York Giants, complained: "That isn't baseball the Orioles are playing. It's an entirely new game."

"It was like an old college football team," McGraw conceded, remembering that he once had gone ten weeks without a rubdown — as though he had just spent ten weeks in the front trenches. His little outfielder, Wee Willie Keeler, was a beady-eyed midget who handled a baseball bat like a pool cue and who once saved a game in Washington by plunging his hand through the barbed wire on top of the fence to catch a long fly ball — though his arm was ripped to the elbow. Another of his head-knockers was Joe Cor-

bett, who once missed spring training because he was moonlighting as the sparring partner of his brother Jim, the heavyweight champion, who once suggested that Joe abandon baseball because it was growing too rough.

But most of McGraw's confidence, as the nineteen twenties arrived, grew from the success that his brand of baseball had bred during his twenty seasons in New York. He had taken over a team that stood eighth and last in the National League, he had bullied it into second place a year later, and he had won the pennant the year after that. Then, for the next twenty years, his teams finished first or second every season but four, and by the time the boys finally marched back home from "Over There" in 1918, the runt from Truxton was king of the biggest hill in professional sports.

One thing began to trouble McGraw, though, as the country slipped into the decade of release that became known as the Roaring Twenties. His team shared its home park, the Polo Grounds, with a tenant — the

Not only that, but they stopped sharing the Polo Grounds
with the Giants late in 1922 and began building their own
park in the Bronx . . .

And as the 1923 baseball season approaches, they rush to finish the most modern park in the business at 161st Street and River Avenue, and from the center-field bleachers you can see forever.

Yankees, who had outgrown their old wooden Hilltop Park in upper Manhattan. The Yankees played in the American League and rivaled the Giants neither in public affection nor public support. But in 1921, one of their players hit fifty-nine home runs. His name was Babe Ruth, and he hit most of them in McGraw's own ball park.

Not only that, but Ruth had hit fifty-four the year before, giving people a chance to talk about something besides the Black Sox scandal of the 1919 World Series. And to make matters worse, McGraw's first baseman, Long George Kelly, unwittingly drew attention to the new phenomenon by leading the National League with only twenty-three home runs.

As if all that weren't enough gall for one man to absorb, the Yankees had begun to pack McGraw's park with their own customers while the Giants were on the road. They drew 619,162 persons in 1919, the year before they pried Ruth from the Boston Red Sox, but when Ruth began to clear McGraw's fences, the tenant's attendance rocketed to 1,289,422. That was double, and McGraw's irritation became triple, especially since the third-place Yankees outdrew the second-place Giants by 100,000.

"The Yankees," he raged to Charles Stoneham, the owner of the Giants, one day, "will have to build a park in Queens or some other out-of-the-way place. Let them go away and wither on the vine."

Withering away on the vine was not exactly what the Yankees had in mind — at least, not the two army colonels who had bought control of the club six years earlier, on January 11, 1915. They may have been a study in contrasts, apart from the coincidence of their military rank — Jacob Ruppert and his spectacularly named partner, Tillinghast l'Hommedieu Huston. But they had one thing in common:

Friends of John McGraw, they had wanted for several years to own a baseball team in New York and had cast eyes at "the" team in town, the Giants. They had been touted instead, by McGraw, to the Yankees. Not only that, but having bought the club, a pig in a poke with World War I bearing down, they charged ahead with a kind of galloping enthusiasm and innocently pledged to give New York an "answer" to the otherwise unanswerable Giants.

They had been born two years apart just after the Civil War, and in most ways that was as close as they came to each other. Ruppert, a dilettante; Huston, earthy and plain. Ruppert, who dressed from an extensive wardrobe with the advice and consent of a valet and tailor; Huston, who wore the same suit

From home plate, wide open spaces . . . and, beyond the
scoreboard, the elevated line brings the crowds uptown.

A gleam in the eye of the Osborn Engineering Company
of Cleveland . . .

THE NEW HOME OF THE AMERICAN LEAGUE BASEBALL CLUB OF NEW YORK
· THE · OSBORN · ENGINEERING · CO · · CLEVELAND ·

for days running, it seemed, and who topped it with a derby that made him, in the words of W. O. McGee-han, "the man in the Iron Hat."

For Ruppert, born in 1867 at Lexington Avenue and 93rd Street on New York's upper East Side, the best was none too good. He was raised into a wealthy beer-brewing family, educated at the Columbia Grammar School, and trained in the Seventh Regiment, the silk-stocking troupe of the New York National Guard. At the age of twenty-two, he was named a colonel by the governor. He owned a town house on Fifth Avenue and an estate on the Hudson River. He collected jade, first editions, race horses, yachts, and Saint Bernard dogs. He was a card-carrying member of the Manhattan Club, the New York Athletic Club, the Catholic Club, the Lambs, and the Liederkranz and Arion Societies. He was one of the most extravagantly eligible bachelors in sight, and he served four terms in Congress besides.

For Huston, who was born in 1869 in a small town

in Ohio, the road took a lot more turns, starting in Cincinnati, where his first job was as the city engineer. When the Spanish-American War began, he organized a regiment of volunteer engineers and marched off as a captain. When it ended, he stayed in Cuba, went into business, and eventually landed the contracts to improve the harbors of Havana, Santiago, and Cienfuegos.

In fact, he met McGraw there during one of the manager's winters-in-the-sun, and they hoisted their way through long evenings at places like the Havana Country Club. Back in New York later, it was McGraw who introduced Huston to Ruppert, crossing their paths somewhere in the vicinity of the Broadway that McGraw ruled by day and by night.

Their most productive meetings were probably by day, in McGraw's ball park, where Ruppert and Huston began to sit together watching the little dictator drive his Giants along. What they also were watching was the changing of the guard, because the Giants had just lost their owner and patron, John T. Brush, something

By air, the battle lines are drawn across the Harlem River.
The world champion Giants live in the horseshoe on
Coogan's Bluff in the upper part of the aerial photo, the
challenging Yankees in the brand-new oval below.

Yankee Stadium opens on April 18, 1923, and six months later the crosstown enemies meet in the main event, the World Series. The first blow is struck by a bow-legged, 33-year-old outfielder for the Giants named Casey Stengel, who hits an inside-the-park home run.

But neither Casey Stengel nor John McGraw nor all the old Giants can withstand the new Goliath of the game, Babe Ruth, who outhits them all.

Miller Huggins, who studied law before becoming master of the Yankees, soon learns to lean on the big man to settle his arguments of the nineteen twenties.

called the Federal League was making hit-and-run raids on the established National and American Leagues, and the "war to end all wars" was breaking out in Europe.

Still, when Ruppert and Huston began asking if they might make a pitch for the Giants, they were told there was no chance for that. However, McGraw, the bosom friend and business shark, replied: "But if you really want to buy a ball club, I think I can get one for you. How about the Yankees?"

In 1915, people were pulling in their financial horns because of the hostilities that were embroiling Europe, but they were still not averse to spending — or making — a fast buck in the States.

The actor John Barrymore, writing a commentary on a book titled *The Broadway That Was*, put it this way: "Broadway has grown smugger. It has grown commonplace and garish. Everybody you see on the street is ready money. If you don't own an automobile, you don't belong on Broadway. It wasn't so in my time."

McGraw, the friend, confidante, and drinking companion of actors the length of Broadway, appreciated the point but did not let it diminish his flair for life. He had just returned a year earlier from a round-the-world tour with his Giants and Charles A. Comiskey's Chicago White Sox — from Cincinnati to Australia to the Pyramids to London. They had traveled 30,000 miles, met the khedive of Egypt and the Pope of Rome, performed before 35,000 Englishmen in one day, and even shaken hands with George V of England, who said: "I am very glad to meet you, Mr. McGraw. Your game is very interesting and I would like to know more about it." To which, McGraw, bowing and retreating to his bench, replied: "We certainly hope that you will have a chance to see more of it."

The free-spending reached a peak back home, mean-

Graham McNamee, a concert baritone, becomes the pioneer voice behind that circular microphone and "the cheers could be heard throughout the land."

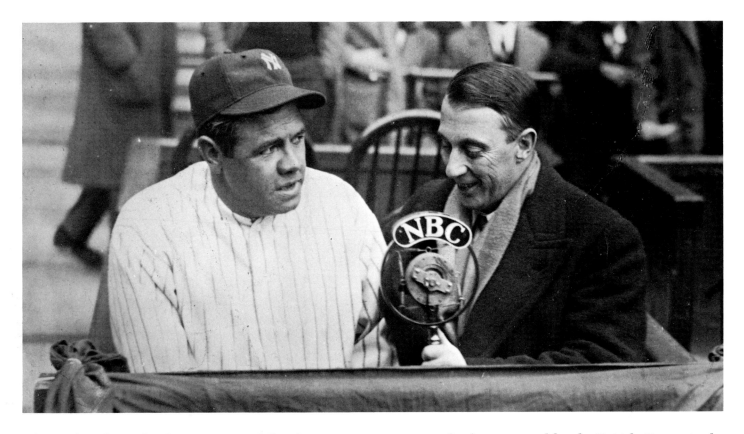

while, when the Federal League started dangling green-backs in front of baseball heroes. Joe Tinker was offered $37,000 for three seasons if he would jump to the Federals, who also offered McGraw $100,000 for one leap, and the Boston Red Sox hurriedly gave Tris Speaker the lordly sum of $37,000 for two years *not* to jump.

So a lot of money was being thrown around despite the stringencies of the war. But one of the things people in 1915 did not do with their money was to spend it on the New York Yankees. Even "risk capital" would have been rated a grave risk in this case because the Yankees were third in a three-horse field then, and the two lead colts were opening daylight on them.

The Giants, running the hottest show in town, operated out of Coogan's Hollow at Eighth Avenue between 155th and 157th Streets in upper Manhattan. Their ball ground, described in real-estate directories as "a four-story structure on City Plot 2106, Lot 100," sat on the

remnant of a farm granted by the British Crown in the seventeenth century to John Lion Gardiner, whose family later settled Gardiners Island off Long Island. The baseball team had moved there in 1889 after a nomad's tour of other vacant lots around the city, from Staten Island to Brooklyn to James Gordon Bennett's polo field at Fifth Avenue and 110th Street, where gentlemen in striped trousers and silk hats would watch the afternoon games. As a result, recalled Meyer Berger in one of his glimpses of New York history, "forever after, the Giants' stadiums were called the Polo Grounds."

The team responded with an unmatched run of success and with an unmatched clientele that on almost any summer afternoon might include the cream of New York's sporting and social life, starting with constant suitors like Ethel Barrymore, who sat meticulously keeping score on a cardboard program before heading

Huge men warming up to play a boy's game: Bob Meusel,
Mark Koenig, Babe Ruth, Lou Gehrig, and Earle Combs,
as the Yankees take over.

Huggins and friends — Waite Hoyt, Ruth, Meusel, and
Bob Shawkey.

There were setbacks, of course, as on October 10, 1926, when old Grover Cleveland Alexander of the St. Louis Cardinals struck out Tony Lazzeri with the bases loaded in the World Series.

downtown for her own performance that evening. Al Jolson would appear on the scene clasping his hands over his head like the heavyweight champion, acknowledging the cheers as he worked his way through the aisles to join George M. Cohan, Eddie Foy, De Wolf Hopper, Jake and Lee Shubert, A. L. Erlanger, William Hammerstein, and even paid-up heavyweight champions like James J. Corbett.

Entranced, the heroes of New York's night life then would watch the heroes of New York's daytime life — Christy Mathewson, Rube Marquard, Josh Devore, Fred Snodgrass, Chief Meyers, and even Jim Thorpe. They drummed fingers to tunes like "Slide, Kelly, Slide" and "Our National Game," which adorned song sheets with intricate line drawings of soap-opera melodramas and even of crossed American flags. And they applauded enthusiastically when McGraw, the star of the cast, would sprint past the outstretched hand of Pants Rowland, the Chicago manager, and snarl: "Get away from me, you damned busher."

Outdistanced in the public passion, but not by much, the Brooklyn Trolley Dodgers held their own sideshow across the East River in Charles H. Ebbets' ball park, the home of one of the more unusual organizations in western civilization.

The Dodgers did not win as often, nor did they earn as much money, as the Giants. But they were staffed by ballplayers who were every bit as eccentric. The team also changed names as frequently as it changed uniforms, starting with the Bridegrooms at the turn of the century — because the club's sizable corps of bachelors somehow had marched to the altar almost en masse during the off season. Later they became the Superbas, because their manager, Ned Hanlon, ran a billiard parlor on the side with the Olympian name of The Superba. Still later, they evolved into the Robins, in tribute to Wilbert Robinson, who had been McGraw's old friend in Baltimore just as strenuously as he became McGraw's personal enemy in New York.

If things ever threatened to grow dull, the situation was regularly saved by hell-raisers like Casey Stengel,

15

September 30, 1927: Tom Zachary of the Washington Senators pitches and George Herman Ruth of the Yankees swings. The home run is number 60 of the season.

the bandy-legged outfielder who joined the Dodgers in 1912 at $2100 a year and who wasted no time making his mark by jumping into the crap game on the locker-room floor. Reprimanded, he went out and made four hits in his major-league debut, then sailed cheerfully ahead as the ringleader of the team's mischief-makers with the richly earned nickname of King of the Grumblers.

"I was fairly good at times," he said later, reviewing his early days in New York's baseball life. "But a lot of people seem to remember some of the stunts I pulled better than they do the ball games I helped win."

But, in a confessional postscript, he conceded with considerable understatement: "I was always in a lot of damn trouble."

Still, it was the third man in town, the Yankees, who suffered the most trouble, chiefly from comparison with their boisterously established neighbors, and it had been that way since they were organized in 1903 as the New York Highlanders.

The main drawback was that they arrived as the new boy on the block, somewhat the way the Jets, the Mets, and the Nets arrived in football, baseball, and basketball half a century later. They were New York's entry in a floundering dream that had been nourished since 1901 by the one-time Cincinnati sportswriter, Byron Bancroft Johnson, the creator of something called the American League.

Johnson crashed his way into the National League's twenty-five-year monopoly with some high cards. He had the financial backing of Ben and Tom Shibe in Philadelphia and of Charles W. Somers in Boston. He had recognized baseball men like Clark Griffith, Charles A. Comiskey, and Connie Mack. He had charter teams in Chicago, Washington, Philadelphia, Cleveland, Detroit, Boston, St. Louis, and Baltimore. He even siphoned off a few players from the National League, which had been in business since 1876. But one thing he did not have was a team in New York, and it didn't take much horse sense to spot the folly of that.

Johnson's first impulse was to switch the celebrated

Orioles from Baltimore to New York with McGraw in charge of the beachhead. But he was foiled by Giant owner John Brush, who spirited McGraw to his home in Indiana one night and signed him on the dining-room table. So McGraw wound up in New York, but Ban Johnson and his new league did not.

Not only that, but through the fall of 1902, Brush kept beating Johnson back from most of the desirable locations for a ball park in Manhattan. He managed that through his partner, Andrew Freedman, who in turn worked through Richard Croker, the fat cat of Tammany Hall, who always stood ready to have new streets cut across any potential American League site.

The two leagues finally met across the table in Cincinnati in January 1903 and worked out a modus vivendi that included New York. They did it without roaring approval from Brush, who still resented any rival in his backyard. But he eventually was outvoted, though he continued to ridicule the idea in public on the unassailable ground that the American League had neither a field for its new club nor a financial angel.

Overnight, though, it found both: Joe Vila, a sportswriter for the *Sun*, had covered the heavyweight title fight between John L. Sullivan and James J. Corbett in New Orleans with Johnson. His circle of friends included Frank Farrell, the one-time bartender and saloonkeeper who had graduated to more exalted things, like running a gambling house and racing stable. With Vila as the go-between, Farrell met Johnson, offered to buy the Baltimore franchise, and backed up the offer with a certified check for $25,000 "as a guarantee of good faith."

When Johnson, with a double-take, observed that "that's a pretty big forfeit, Mr. Farrell," his doubts were eased by Vila, who reported: "He bets that much on a horse race."

Farrell added that he would be partners with William S. Devery, whose nickname in an era of nicknames was "Big Bill," also a one-time bartender who had contemplated a career as either a prize fighter or policeman. He settled on the latter, rose to head the depart-

The home-run twins, Ruth and Lou Gehrig, fishing together
off Florida in spring training . . .

. . . and playing ball together in the stadium, a familiar pose
as Gehrig welcomes Ruth home after his record-setting
sixtieth home run in 1927.

ment, retired somehow with plenty of money, and then turned his talent to real estate. They had, Farrell noted, a good location for the ball club: "It runs from One hundred sixty-fifth Street to One hundred sixty-eighth Street on Broadway." To which Johnson replied, still unconvinced: "That's a long way uptown."

But the deal was made, the partners bought the Baltimore franchise for $18,000, the team was shifted to New York, Clark Griffith was hired as manager, and Farrell and Devery agreed to buy the property on Broadway and build a park there in time for the 1903 season.

Brush and Freedman, the partners in the other camp, flinched at the prospect of an instant rival and responded in the time-honored manner: They threatened

to have streets cut through the site. But Farrell and Devery rode out the threat, realizing that Croker was losing his bite with Tammany and also realizing that they had the support of their own political tigers like Big Tim Sullivan, Little Tim Sullivan, and Tom Foley. In three months' time, like cattle ranchers driving off the sheep men, they turned loose crews of workers, leveling the land, scraping it smooth, building a wooden grandstand and bleachers with 15,000 seats and a wooden clubhouse, and circling the property with a wooden fence.

They named Joseph W. Gordon, a mild-mannered coal merchant, as president — partly for window-dressing — and introduced their team as the Highlanders. It was a play on words, because the team performed

He was "Columbia's ace pitcher" the day Yankee Stadium opened in 1923, but before the season was over, Henry Louis Gehrig had joined the Yankees. Two years later, he got into the line-up regularly — for 2130 games in a row.

May 2, 1939: The Iron Man's streak ends in Detroit.

He was fatally sick, but still smiling, as he hung up number 4 for the last time.

He was, he said, the luckiest man on the face of the earth.

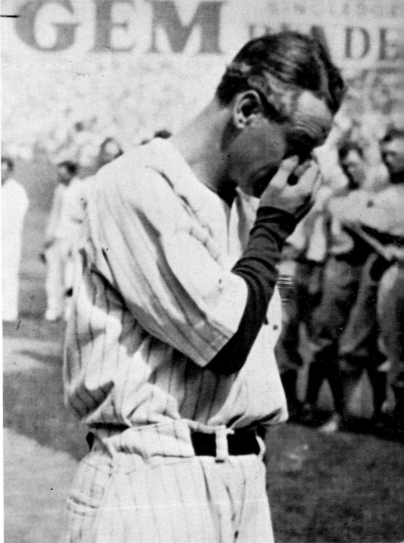

In the nineteen thirties, their names were Joe DiMaggio, Frank Crosetti, Tony Lazzeri, Bill Dickey, Lou Gehrig, Jake Powell, and George Selkirk. What they had in common with the Yankees of Ruth's day was those bats.

The 1937 infield: Gehrig, Lazzeri, Crosetti, and Red Rolfe.

LEFT   He arrived in 1936 and for the next fifteen seasons led the charge — Joe D.

BELOW   June 29, 1941: The hitting streak reaches 42 consecutive games, and the dugout meets the man. He kept hitting, too, until the streak reached 56 games.

on one of the highest spots in Manhattan and because Gordon's Highlanders then were probably the best-known regiment in the British army. They made their debut in Washington on April 22, 1903, losing to the Senators by 3 to 1, and then opened in New York on May 1. Marching bands gave out with "Columbia, the Gem of the Ocean" and "Yankee Doodle." Jack Chesbro pitched for the home side. Willie Keeler contributed two walks, two doubles, and three runs and in the out-field almost fell into a ravine while chasing a fly ball. It was the Highlanders, 6 to 2, over Washington, and the American League had made New York.

One year later, the Highlanders even advanced to the brink of the league's pennant but lost it on the final day to the Boston Red Sox when Chesbro threw a wild pitch that let in the deciding run. But they at least won the satisfaction of ruffling the feathers of the old Oriole, McGraw, who decided not to dignify the new league by allowing his Giants to meet it in the World Series.

Seven years later, though, a fire at the Polo Grounds left the Giants homeless and the Highlanders took them into their own park as tenants until the damage was repaired. It was a long stride forward in the pecking order. Two years after that, the Giants returned the favor, offering them house room in the larger and grander Polo Grounds, and the Highlanders left their little old park for a fancier address.

They had a fancier name, too. By 1913, sports editors around town found headline space too confining for eleven-letter words like "Highlanders" and began to coin synonyms. The move from the Hilltop to the hollow provided the final flourish and, when the team pitched camp in the Polo Grounds, the calling card read "New York Yankees."

"How about the Yankees?" John McGraw was asking Ruppert and Huston in 1915 when the two colonels intensified their shopping for a baseball club.

Like all Giant fans, and like most businessmen, Ruppert and Huston weren't too interested. To them, the Giants were still the only team in town and the Giants' horde of public admirers formed the only swinging circle of fans in town. But McGraw, as soft on cronies as he was brutal on rivals, kept working on them, and they finally checked with Farrell — who by now was getting short on cash and long on arguments with Devery.

As a result, Ruppert and Huston anted up $460,000, which Farrell and Devery split. Then Farrell and Devery just plain split, taking their money and going sep-

arate ways until Devery died in 1919 and Farrell in 1926. They ended pretty much where they had started: Farrell left an "estate" of just $1072. Devery left $2500 — which had been paid by Harry M. Stevens for catering rights at the Hilltop park and which for some reason he had never touched.

The papers were signed on January 11, 1915, putting Ruppert and Huston in control of their pig in a poke. They still shared McGraw's ball park and they still shared McGraw's favor. But they didn't share his ranking along Broadway. And so, drawing a bead on the only worthwhile target in town, they opened shop with the lofty but quaint notion that they would offer New York an "answer" to the otherwise unanswerable Giants.

D own on the Potomac, close by the National Capitol, they are thinking about erecting an impressive monument to the national game of baseball," the *New York Times* reported on April 18, 1923, in the cheerleading tone of the day. "But in the busy borough of the Bronx, close to the shore of Manhattan island, the real monument to baseball will be unveiled this afternoon — the new Yankee Stadium, erected at a cost of $2,500,000, seating some 70,000 people and comprising in its broad reaches of concrete and steel the last word in baseball arenas.

"Today's the day for the dyed-in-the-wool fans, for office boys with delicate grandparents and for baseball sportsmen everywhere. But it means even a little more than this to friends of the Yankees, who have been waiting for this day ever since the American Leaguers packed bag and baggage and moved out of that antiquated wooden home of theirs on Washington Heights back in 1912."

It was a monument, all right, but if anything it was a monument to the ambition of Jacob Ruppert and Tillinghast l'Hommedieu Huston after they had bought the ball club eight years earlier. It was also a monument to the ambition of their friend John McGraw, who had expansively suggested the investment — but who now had reason to regret his expansiveness.

At that, the two colonels had been forced to struggle during those eight years before building a monument to anything outside of their own folly. When they took over the team, they literally had two strikes on them: no team to speak of and no place of their own to display it. Then World War I broke out, Huston joined the expeditions overseas, and now he and his partner were an ocean apart with two strikes on them.

They also didn't have a manager for their orphan team, which was threatening to become an expensive hobby, even for a pair of well-heeled enthusiasts. But far worse, they had no dramatic figure on the field who might challenge McGraw's men for the grip they had held on the public imagination for almost a generation. At the turnstiles, where expensive hobbies became expensive business, that was more urgent than any other minus sign.

As the Highlanders, the Yankees already had gone the distance on managers. They had started with a tried-and-true baseball name, Clark Griffith, for five seasons and a fraction. Then six managers in the next six years, beginning with Kid Elberfeld in 1908, and including George Stallings, later the miracle worker of the 1914 Boston Braves; Hal Chase, the stylish first baseman who came closest to being the team's public hero; Frank Chance, the anchor of the old double-play legend with Joe Tinker and Johnny Evers; and Harry Wolverton, fresh from the Tri-State League, who wore a sombrero and smoked long cigars.

Finally, in 1918, while Ruppert and Huston were still firing messages to each other across the Atlantic, a name was dropped onto the table by Ban Johnson — Miller J. Huggins, the one-time shortstop in the Western League who had been running the St. Louis Cardinals for the last five years. Huggins was a small, wiry man who had studied law during the off season and who had been admitted to the bar. He also owned a piece of the St. Louis club and wasn't too interested

27

From 1931 to 1946, the man in the dugout was Joseph Vincent McCarthy, a Philadelphian who had never played in the big leagues. Eight pennants later, the cry of "Break up the Yankees" was heard in the land.

in switching. But he and Ruppert hit it off after they were introduced and, although Huston disavowed the selection in another message from overseas, the club hired Huggins in 1918 and for the next dozen years he was the man in the dugout.

More important, aside from any talent Huggins might have focused on the Yankees, the owners began to lavish cash on their hobby. Attendance limped along to 282,047 in 1918 and then, as the Armistice released the men and money in 1919, it soared to 619,164. But that could be traced to a sort of historical imperative, and not to the presence of any towering figure on the field. They did spend $40,000 to buy Carl Mays, the pitcher who fired fast balls underhanded. But the league president cast a pall over the deal by accusing Mays of having provoked a suspension in Boston so that the Red Sox would unload him squarely onto the greener fields of New York.

There was another rub: People paid their way into ball parks primarily to watch somebody sock a ball with a baseball bat. The best average on the Yankees was .305, and what they clearly needed was a big man with bat to match.

George Herman Ruth was the name — a strapping teen-ager in blue overalls at St. Mary's Industrial School in Baltimore, a catcher who threw left-handed, who also pitched and swung left-handed, and who did all three better than anybody in town. He was signed right out of school by Jack Dunn, president and manager of the Orioles, who became his father image as well as his employer. So much so, that when Ruth appeared for the first time in the Orioles training camp as a nineteen-year-old, he was Jack's boy, Jack's baby — the Babe.

He slipped into the big leagues when Dunn sold him to Boston, which farmed him out to Providence of the International League. He pitched some days, played the outfield on others. He was recalled by the Red Sox in September, pitched four times, won twice and lost once. It was 1914, and the next year, while Ruppert and

Sixty years of Yankee history in six managers: Bucky Harris,
Bob Shawkey, Clark Griffith, Joe McCarthy, Casey Stengel,
and Roger Peckinpaugh.

They could break your heart lots of ways. The date is
October 5, 1941; the batter striking out is Tommy Henrich;
the catcher is Mickey Owen; the umpire, Larry Goetz. It
should have ended the game, but before the inning was
over, the Yankees had devastated the Brooklyn Dodgers,
7 to 4.

Huston were taking over the Yankees in New York, Jack
Dunn's baby was winning eighteen games in Boston.

A year later, he won twenty-three, defeated the
Dodgers in the World Series, and came back to win
twenty-four the year after that. Then, in 1918, while
Ruppert and Huston were firing salvos across the ocean
trying to untrack their new ball club, he pitched thirteen
victories plus two in the World Series — and hit eleven
home runs, besides.

By then, Jack Dunn's baby had long since become
the hottest topic in the dugouts and front offices of
baseball, an improbable hybrid who ranked simultaneously as the best left-handed pitcher in the American
League and the best power hitter, even part-time. So
in the spring of 1919, the general manager of the Red
Sox, Edward Grant Barrow, cast the die. He could
have Ruth every fourth day as a pitcher or every day
as a hitter. He elected the long ball, sacrificed the
frontline pitcher, and made history. Ruth promptly hit
.322 with twenty-nine home runs, a record for both
leagues, and the postwar crowds began to flock to the
park to see him powder the ball — including Ruppert
and Huston.

The Red Sox were owned then by Harry Frazee, a
one-time bill poster from Peoria whose weakness still
was the theater. It was a runaway weakness, too, because he kept losing money on shows that flopped —
while Ruth started to attract money with his towering
home runs. But Frazee's actors were emptying his
pockets faster than his ballplayers could fill them, and
he went broke again despite the fact that he owned
the greatest show in sports.

He turned to New York for help, asking Ruppert to
lend him half a million dollars, and the colonel coun-
tered with trump: Ruth. That was a horse of another
color, so Frazee hustled back to Boston and put it to
Barrow, who pointed out that none of the Yankee players, individually or collectively, was worth taking in
exchange for Ruth. However, he added, if Frazee really
needed the money to stay in business, he had no choice
but to cash in his one gold nugget at the highest price
available.

Frazee agreed, accepting $100,000 in cash plus a
personal loan of $350,000 from Ruppert; the colonel took
a mortgage on Fenway Park as collateral and the Yankees got Babe Ruth.

But there were times when the Dodgers had their inning, as in the 1947 Series when Al Gionfriddo robbed DiMaggio of a big one.

As with any earthquake, the tremors were felt in all directions for a long time. They were felt, first of all, by the Giants — who had scheduled a spring-training tour with the Red Sox because of Ruth's drawing power. Now they had to take the tour without him while the Yankees were raking in the chips on the road ahead of them with their new boy wonder. Not only that, but when the regular season opened, the Yankees were still sharing the Polo Grounds and the Giants now had Ruth under their own roof on somebody else's payroll.

The main tremors, though, were felt by the Yankees, who charged ahead after eighteen years of wandering, just missed winning a pennant for the first time, and doubled their home attendance to 1,289,422. Ruth finished the season with the fourth highest batting average in the league at .376 and raised the roof for all time with fifty-four home runs.

The tremors were still being felt that fall, when Barrow — the man who had touched them off — also switched to the Yankees as business manager. He was fifty-two years old then, a tall and husky man from a farm in Illinois, and he already had worn more hats in baseball than most. He had worked with Harry Stevens, the caterer; had helped form the Interstate League; had served as a manager at Wheeling, West Virginia, and had won the pennant there; had managed at Paterson, New Jersey, in 1896; had run the Detroit Tigers; had organized the International League in 1910; and had wound up in 1918 as manager of the Red Sox, who immediately won the pennant in his first season as boss.

With the Yankees late in 1920, Barrow quickly swung an eight-player trade — or raid — with his old club in Boston, acquiring Waite Hoyt and Wally Schang for his new club in New York. And in 1923, he picked off Herb Pennock from the Red Sox. The Yankees, meanwhile, had finally made it to the top of the American League by taking the pennant in 1921 and 1922. They were beaten back in the World Series both years, though, by the Giants, leaving McGraw still in control of the Battle of Broadway. But McGraw needed no

Casey Stengel, who returned to the scene as manager of the Yankees in 1949, peers into his crystal ball . . .

. . . and what he sees usually turns out to be cause for rejoicing.

In the Professor's case, beauty is in the eye of the beholder.

One of Casey's old antagonists, Rogers Hornsby, could do
tricks with a baseball, too — like hitting it.

September 28, 1951, Allie Reynolds is one pitch from completing his second no-hitter of the season. The pitch is delivered to Ted Williams, who lifts a high foul not far from the dugout . . .

reminders that the tide, and the clamor, were tilting toward his tenant. He began to apply the pressure, suggesting that the Yankees find some other home where they might "wither on the vine," while the *New York Times* marked the changing of the guard in 1922 in these words:

"Radio for the first time carried the opening game of the World Series, play by play, direct from the Polo Grounds to great crowds throughout the eastern section of the country. Through the broadcasting station WJZ at Newark, New Jersey, Grantland Rice, a sportswriter, related his story of the game direct to an invisible audience, estimated to be five million, while WGY at Schenectady and WBZ at Springfield, Massachusetts, relayed every play of the contest.

"In place of the scoreboards and megaphones of the past, amplifiers connected to radio instruments gave all the details and sidelights to thousands of enthusiasts unable to get into the Polo Grounds. Not only could the voice of the official radio observer be heard, but the voice of the umpire on the field announcing the batteries for the day mingled with the voice of a boy selling ice cream cones.

"The clamor of the 40,000 baseball fans inside the Polo Grounds made radio listeners feel as if they were in the grandstand. The cheers which greeted Babe Ruth when he stepped to the plate could be heard throughout the land . . ."

April 18, 1923, was a cool and somewhat cloudy day in New York. "It is apt to be a bit chilly during the opening game of the baseball season," Macy's predicted in its newspaper ads that morning, thoughtfully adding that newly arrived topcoats (at $27.50 to $54.75) might be a good idea, "especially near the close of the game." Or, perhaps a cap (at $1.88) or Lansdowne hat ($4.89). And, as an afterthought, "Take along plenty of smokes, and we suggest the following items to add to your en-

. . . Yogi Berra, a man with good hands, come a little undone as he chases the "final out," which winds up on the grass along with Yogi. However, Williams then helps Berra redeem himself by hitting an identical foul ball, which Yogi grabs without acrobatics.

joyment of the National Game: Tampa blunts ($2.49 for a can of fifty), made with Havana filler and Havana wrapper; Italian briar pipes (thirty-nine cents apiece); or Three Castles cigarettes, packed in airtight tins of fifty each (at $1.88)."

Altman & Company shared Macy's concern for the outdoor fan, offering "New Motor Robes, which will harmonize effectively with the upholstery in cars of the better makes" and "variously priced from $10.50 to $47.50." Best & Company also joined in the concern sweeping the midtown stores, getting right to the point in its ads: "Going to the game? You'll need a new top-coat and you'll want it to be English, *of course*. You can pay more but you don't need to. Prices start at $36." And Wallach Brothers, placing its stress on the subtle-ties of the day, made a pitch for Gage roll-front Arrow collars "that will meet the young man's fancy of what a low collar should be — easy flowing in lines, comfort-able in wear, very easy on the cravat knot," and all that for just twenty cents apiece.

A lot of people, admittedly, might decide to spend their time indoors and forgo the season's bargains. After all, Richard Barthelmess and Dorothy Gish were appearing at the Strand in the film *The Bright Shawl*, and Pola Negri was at the Rivoli in *Bella Donna*, while Gloria Swanson was holding forth at the Rialto in *Prodigal Daughters*. Or, for those who might cling to live entertainment despite the new flicks, there was always *Abie's Irish Rose* at the Republic, Lionel Atwill in *The Comedian* at the Lyceum, H. B. Warner in *You and I* at the Belmont, and the Ziegfeld Follies at the New Amsterdam. Or, combining past and present, Rupert Hughes could be seen at the Capitol Theatre delivering a lecture on "the art of the motion picture."

There was also the S.S. *Leviathan* Orchestra of the United States Lines, the same orchestra that would "furnish music on the world's largest ship," now open-ing at Keith's Palace "under the exclusive management of Paul Whiteman."

But for the music lover who also fancied live actors as well as those imported English topcoats, the place to be was the new ball yard in town — Yankee Stadium, where the Seventh Regiment Band serenaded what the press acclaimed as "the greatest crowd that ever saw a baseball game."

"Governors, generals, colonels, politicians and base-

ball officials gathered together solemnly to dedicate the biggest stadium in baseball," the *Times* reported. "By official count, 74,200 people were inside the grounds. Outside the park, flattened against doors that had long since closed, were 20,000 more fans who finally turned around and went home, convinced that baseball parks are not nearly as large as they should be."

This particular park covered ten acres in the Bronx, between 157th and 161st Streets, from River Avenue to Doughty. It had been bought on February 5, 1921, from the estate of William Waldorf Astor by Ruppert and Huston, who presumably were two of the colonels the *Times* had spied in the opening-day throng. The running time from Forty-second Street by subway, the Yankees noted, with one eye on the Giants across the river in upper Manhattan, was "about sixteen minutes." And the events unfolding inside would be made "impenetrable to all human eyes, save those of aviators, by towering embattlements."

The embattlements probably represented a slight case of poetic license, but most of the other architectural glories of the stadium passed the test. The builder, the White Construction Company, recorded its role in the corporate archives in proud language that might just as well have portrayed the saga of the Suez Canal or the Great Wall of China.

This is the story — briefly told — about the construction of the largest baseball stadium in America.

It is about the building in twelve months of a three-deck, reinforced-concrete and structural-steel grandstand and over 40,000 square feet of wooden bleachers for the American League Base Ball Club of New York, Inc., more familiarly known as the "Yankees."

The Yankee Stadium, as it is called, is more than a ball park. It is an office building — a main restaurant with several branches — a club house complete in itself — an athletic field subdrained by 25,000 running feet of clay pipe.

In April, 1922, the owners came to "White" and said, "We own a plot of ground up in the Bronx, at 161st Street and River Avenue, containing about 240,000 square feet. We *must* play ball there next spring. The Osborne Engineering Co. of Cleveland, Ohio, are preparing the plans and specifications for a stand that will seat about 75,000. The contractor that we will eventually select must furnish everything, even the 'home plate' and the laundry equipment. We are going to let this business at a definite price — a

37

LEFT   The little magician at shortstop in the nineteen fifties was Phil Rizzuto, doing his thing here in the 1951 World Series against the New York Giants. Alvin Dark bites the dust while Gerry Coleman roots.

BELOW   The Yankees got used to Rizzuto's tricks with a glove, but when he hit a home run in the 1951 Series, they flipped.

They could beat you with their gloves, too . . .

lump-sum basis — and we must have the completed stadium by April 18th, 1923. Are you interested?" We were.

On May 5th, the work was awarded to the White Construction Co., Inc., on the basis mentioned above. Two hundred eighty-four working days later, the park was turned over to the owners, but what an undertaking that was. During the course of construction, the owners made numerous changes in the structure, which necessarily delayed the progress of the work. Strikes, on and away from the site, slowed down the work or stopped temporarily the manufacture of material needed in the building. There was no penalty or bonus attached to the contract, but there was a definite moral obligation to finish on time. We had promised; *we knew that we must finish on time.*

What this meant may be gained from the following facts:

Before any appreciable amount of construction work could be done, 45,000 cubic yards of earth had to be transported in motor trucks to rough-grade the property.

Nine hundred and fifty thousand board feet of Pacific Coast fir were brought via the Panama Canal to erect the bleachers.

To erect the stadium proper, over three million board feet of temporary form work was required, twenty thousand cubic yards of concrete and eight hundred tons of reinforcing steel.

Twenty-two hundred tons of structural steel had to be fabricated and erected.

The playing field has over thirteen thousand cubic yards of top soil and is covered with one hundred and sixteen thousand square feet of sod.

The seats in the grandstand were manufactured at the site, and required one hundred thirty-five thousand individual steel castings, four hundred thousand pieces of maple lumber, secured to the castings with over one million brass screws. The seats were expansion-bolted to the decks and necessitated the drilling of over ninety thousand holes in the concrete.

As if all that weren't breathtaking enough for one project, White's official history of the undertaking also noted that the copper frieze at the top of the façade inside the stadium was sixteen feet in depth. Also, and this may have been the most remarkable feat of all,

... though sometimes tricky little pop flies almost made history. Jackie Robinson hit this pop fly in the final game of the 1952 Series and it almost causes havoc until Billy Martin dashes in from second base to save the day.

"such a gigantic undertaking" was completed "in so short a time on a fixed-cost basis."

When the gates were opened at noon on that Wednesday in April, only 500 pioneers were lined up for their first glimpse. By two o'clock, though, the gates were closed again to keep anybody else from crashing in, and by three o'clock people were saying that the great crowd exceeded "the Boston record" by 30,000.

The High Commissioner of Baseball, the former federal judge named Kenesaw Mountain Landis, traveled to the scene in what the newspapers decided was "democratic style." He took the Interborough subway. When he disembarked shortly before two o'clock, at the height of the storming-of-the-gates, he was trapped in a swirl of bodies and finally had to be rescued by the police and escorted inside. As he was, two men were arrested outside and were fined for having offered a city detective a $1.10 grandstand seat for $1.25 and another for $1.50. They were accused of having violated Section 1534 of the Penal Law and were held in $500 bail for trial as speculators. Nobody seemed to think it was far-fetched that they had been peddling the tickets so cheaply.

Inside the park, the Seventh Regiment Band kept up the beat while Governor Alfred E. Smith and his wife made their way to the front box reserved for Landis, a gray-hawk figure in gray overcoat and wide-brimmed hat, who three years earlier had hurled retribution at the eight members of the Chicago White Sox implicated in "fixing" the 1919 World Series. Mayor John Hylan was absent because he was ill, and so was Ban Johnson because of a sudden attack of the flu. But Charles A. Stoneham represented the Giants, who were off in Boston beating the Braves for the second time in a row, 7 to 4; and Harry Frazee represented the visiting Red Sox with the mixed emotions of a rival who has contributed extravagantly to somebody else's prosperity.

Now at three o'clock, the Yankees appeared in their white home uniforms and the Red Sox in their gray, with red sweaters, red caps, and red-striped stockings. They headed for the third-base side of the infield, in front of

In the 1955 Series, though, the saver is supplied for the Dodgers by Sandy Amoros on a ball hit by Berra.

the Yankee dugout, while John Philip Sousa, in bandmaster's finery, took baton in hand and stepped to the head of the company. With Sousa and the band leading the way, the teams and the political lions paraded to the center-field flagpole, marching across the 13,000 cubic yards of topsoil and 116,000 square feet of new sod while the crowd rustled to its feet.

First, the National Anthem while the American flag was hoisted; then the Yankees' pennant of 1922. And, the *Times* reported, "The big crowd let loose a roar that floated across the Harlem and far beyond."

Back toward home plate they marched again, now with Colonels Ruppert and Huston leading the way, followed by Landis, Frazee, and Al Smith, who triggered the main event by throwing out the first ball. It was caught by Wally Schang, the Yankee catcher, who then started aiming his mitt toward Bob Shawkey.

For the people who chronicled the rest of the afternoon's events, everything seemed to rise to heroic dimensions. There was Shawkey, "the war veteran and oldest Yankee player in point of service," pitching "the finest game of his career, letting the Boston batters down with three scattered hits." There was Everett Scott, the shortstop, playing in his nine-hundred-eighty-seventh game in a row despite an ankle that had been sprained during an exhibition at Springfield, Missouri. There were Whitey Witt, Joe Dugan, Bob Meusel, and all the regulars who had challenged McGraw for two seasons for the big money.

There was Jack Dunn's baby, too, generously quoted before the game as saying he would give a year of his roistering life to hit the first home run in the park. And there he was in the third inning, hitting the two and two pitch from Howard Ehmke ten rows back into the right-field seats *for* the first home run. Ehmke, the press exulted, "tried to fool him with one of those slow balls that the Giants used successfully in the last World Series." But Ruth gathered himself and gave it the roundhouse swing with Witt leading off third base and Dugan off first.

The script was almost too good to be true. An inning

October 8, 1956: Twenty-seven outs in a row by a 27-year-
old pitcher named Don Larsen . . .

. . . All alone and lonely, Jake Pitler, the first-base coach for the Dodgers, with absolutely nobody to talk to . . .

. . . Berra, who called the signals, approves . . .

. . . and, a few seconds later, so does everybody in sight.

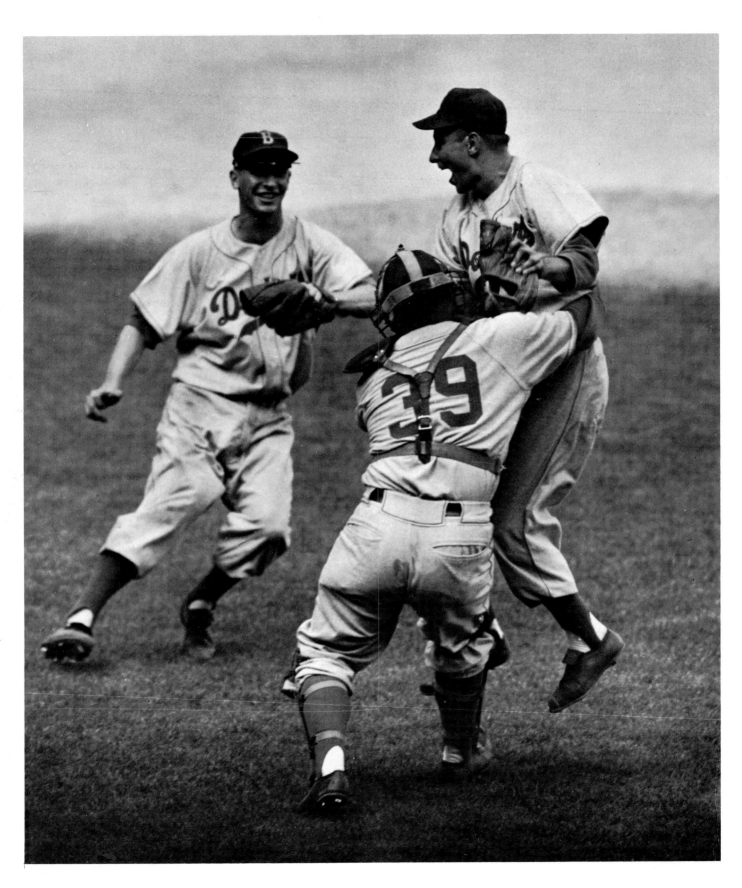

against a left-handed hitter, and up in the press box the ball was watched by Frederick G. Lieb, one of the pioneer baseball writers, who remembered later: "I didn't think the ball was hit too hard. It looked to me like a single."

But the ball skipped through the alley in left-center on two bounces and caromed off the fence 450 feet from home plate, reminding everybody how spacious the new ball park really was — especially Meusel and Witt, who were chasing the ball. But their ordeal was nothing compared with Stengel's. As he circled the bases, Casey realized that he represented the tie-breaking run, but he also realized that his gimpy old legs might resign from the mission before it was completed. And years later, he recalled saying — or thinking — to himself, as the crowd of 55,307 followed him around the bases with roars: "Go, legs, go; drive this boy around the bases."

Rounding third, he half lost a shoe, but he staggered along anyway as Meusel fired the long relay to Scott, and Scott in turn fired it home to Wally Schang while Stengel, one shoe flopping and both feet dragging, pitched himself toward the plate. High over the scene, watching in the vicinity of Fred Lieb, sat Damon Runyon, who portrayed it in these words in one of the early pieces of lore evoked in Jacob Ruppert's new stadium:

This is the way old Casey Stengel ran yesterday afternoon running his home run home.

This is the way old Casey Stengel ran running his home run home to a Giant victory by a score of 5 to 4 in the first game of the World Series of 1923.

This is the way old Casey Stengel ran running his home run home when two were out in the ninth inning and the score was tied, and the ball still bounding inside the Yankee yard.

This is the way —

His mouth wide open.

His warped old legs bending beneath him at every stride.

His arms flying back and forth like those of a man swimming with a crawl stroke.

His flanks heaving, his breath whistling, his head far back. Yankee infielders, passed by Old Casey Stengel as he was running his home run home, say Casey was muttering to himself, adjuring himself to greater speed as a jockey mutters to his horse in a race, saying: "Go on, Casey, go on."

The warped old legs, twisted and bent by many a year of baseball campaigning, just barely held out under Casey until he reached the plate, running his home run home.

Then they collapsed.

Two days later, Casey was back in center field and the Series was back in Yankee Stadium after a one-day switch to the Polo Grounds. The Yankees had recovered their poise, and Stengel had recovered his breath during the second game, while Herb Pennock pitched them to victory over the Giants and Ruth trumped Casey's ace by hitting *two* home runs. But now, for the third game, a record Series crowd of 62,450 packed the park and watched Sad Sam Jones shut out the Giants for six innings and Art Nehf shut out the Yankees for six.

This time, as Stengel advanced to the plate, he was greeted by a solid wall of booing, hooting, and catcalling from the Yankee bench, in tribute to his theatrical performance of forty-eight hours earlier. This time, he responded in the only sensible way for a man determined not to run around those bases again in a dead heat with Bob Meusel's rifle arm. He lifted one of Sad Sam's pitches into the right-field seats for his second home run of the Series and punctuated the feat by artfully thumbing his nose in the general direction of the home team's dugout.

"I made out like a bee or fly was bothering me," he said later, nailing the point for posterity. "So I kept rubbing the end of my nose, with my fingers pointed toward the Yankee dugout."

Among those not amused by the trick was Ruppert, who indignantly hurried to the Commissioner's box and told Landis that Stengel had insulted players and fans alike (besides beating the Yankees, 1 to 0).

"I heard about that in a hurry," Stengel recalled. "Landis called me over and said he didn't like that kind of exhibition before sixty thousand people, and he told me, 'If you do that again, I promise you one thing: You won't receive a dollar of your World Series share.'"

To punctuate the point, Landis fined him fifty dollars on the spot, though Stengel did not learn until later that

LEFT Mantle and DiMaggio — for thirty years, one or the other patrolled center field most days. Between them, 897 home runs.

BELOW What so proudly we hailed . . .

May 22, 1963: Space shot. Bill Fischer of Kansas City was the pitcher, Mantle the batter, and the ball just missed going all the way out. Tape-measure specialists calculated it would have traveled 620 feet if it had not bounced off the upper-deck façade. To Mantle: "the hardest ball I ever hit."

August 12, 1964: Another space shot. This one, off Ray Herbert of Chicago, clears the screen in center field with Gene Stephens in pursuit.

the Commissioner had refused sterner punishment and had put off the furious Ruppert by observing: "Well, Casey Stengel just can't help being Casey Stengel."

As it turned out, Babe Ruth couldn't help being Babe Ruth, either. He hit *three* home runs in the Series, and the only two games the Giants won were won by Stengel's two homers. Casey, pocketing a loser's share of $4112, was traded to the Boston Braves before the winter had passed; Ruth, pocketing a winner's share of $6143, towered higher than before over the Broadway that had belonged unchallenged to McGraw and his Giants.

Built for baseball, built supposedly "for" one baseball player, the new stadium in the Bronx almost immediately gave New York a new stage — and across it paraded the people, politicians, pastors, and professionals of the tumultuous twenties. Three months after the Yankees and Red Sox had played the first ball game in it, Leonard and Tendler fought for the first championship in it, in a ring set up near second base, the first of twenty-nine title fights that extended from Harry Greb to Gene Tunney to Henry Armstrong and Sugar Ray Robinson down to the days almost four decades later of Ingemar Johansson and Floyd Patterson — with Joe Lewis and Max Schmeling providing the two most memorable nights of all.

It was a time of sports idols, of a hippodrome atmosphere that entwined the great and the small of the theater, racetracks, the courts, the political clubs, and even the underworld, all somehow interlocked as the demigods of public life in the stampede away from World War I.

"The vandals sacking Rome," observed Gene Fowler, "were ten times as kindly as the spendthrift hordes on Broadway. The Wall Street delirium was reaching the pink-elephant stage. Chambermaids and counter-hoppers had the J. P. Morgan complex. America had the swelled head, and the brand of tourists that went to Europe became ambassadors of ill-will. The World War killed nearly everything that was old Broadway.

Thirty-four years after Babe Ruth hit 60, Roger Maris hits 60. The date is September 26, 1961; the pitcher, Jack Fisher of Baltimore . . .

Prohibition, the mock-turtle soup of purists, provided the *coup de grâce.*"

The "era of wonderful nonsense," they called it, the world rushing downhill on a bicycle and raising the roof en route. A time of Eve Curie and John D. Rockefeller, of criminals like Arnold Rothstein and of criminal lawyers like William J. Fallon, suave and smooth and supereloquent, who once was asked if he had been drinking by a teetotaling judge during a huddle before the bench. To which Fallon replied, in the spirit of the time: "If Your Honor's sense of justice is as good as his sense of smell, my client need have no worry in this court."

It was a time when celebrated critics like Alexander Woollcott might watch an Actors Equity review, decide it was a "show of strength," and then portray it in the *New York Times* in these ringing words:

"Here, for instance, was John Barrymore, a pallid, rose-clad Romeo, looking unutterably romantic to the last as the ruthless elevator withdrew him from sight. Here was Laurette Taylor, all loveliness as Ophelia, and Lionel Atwill, looking twice as melancholy and several times as Danish as the usual Hamlet. Here was Chrystal Herne, allowed just a moment to suggest how enchanting a Viola she might be, and Jane Cowl as the Shrew glaring defiance at the amiable Petruchio of John Drew.

"Here was Doris Keane playing Portia to the evil-looking Shylock of George Arliss, and here was Genevieve Tobin, a most delicate Ariel, dancing before the Prospero of Frank Bacon. There was no fairer vision than that which Peggy Wood presented as Imogen — an hour of *Cymbeline* after two years of *Buddies.*

"It was, in a sense, a night of reunions, for here was Lillian Russell resplendent as Queen Katherine and such old favorites as James T. Powers and Rose Coghlan to show that Equity was no mere enthusiasm of the youngsters. But between these old-timers and such stars of tomorrow as the Duncan sisters, the audience was all affable impartiality. When these frivolous newcomers did their turn, there was wild applause."

. . . and number 61. The date is October 1; the pitcher,
Tracy Stallard of Boston . . .

There was wild applause, also, for football heroes like Red Grange, who single-handedly rescued the five-year-old National Football League in 1925 — twenty teams sprawled around the landscape from Providence to Kansas City, with only Chicago and New York of any consequence in size and money. Then, a few days after Grange's final game as an undergraduate for the University of Illinois, he was signed by George Halas for his Chicago Bears. Not only signed, but transported around the country in a whirlwind tour as an attraction, like King Kong, while the dollars were counted by Grange's agent, a theater operator from Champaign, Illinois, with the absolutely appropriate name of C. C. Pyle — Cash & Carry Pyle.

They started in Wrigley Field, where the Bears played the Chicago Cardinals on Thanksgiving Day before a sellout crowd of 36,000 persons, in a day when football did not play to sellout crowds. Then on to St. Louis, where Grange scored four touchdowns and 8000 persons paid; to Philadelphia, two more touchdowns and 35,000 more customers; to New York, another touchdown and the jackpot of 65,000 admissions; to Washington, where he kicked two field goals before 8000 more; and so on to Boston, Detroit, and back to Chicago. Then, a month later, to Coral Gables, Florida, in knickers, loud socks, and special sweaters with "Bears" embroidered across the front, charging as much as $19.80 for a single ticket. And as they turned into January, on to New Orleans, Los Angeles, San Diego, San Francisco, Portland, and Seattle.

They sometimes exaggerated the size of the gate, but nobody exaggerated the size of the take — 360,000 customers in twenty games for a net of a quarter of a million dollars. And to Halas, who had started as general manager, publicity man, ticket seller, and star end of the bears, the stadiums and the crowds were here to stay.

Even the crowned heads of Europe and their relatives joined the fun. After watching the storied Meadowbrook polo team on Long Island for two days, Lord Louis Mountbatten and his bride decided to accept Ruppert's invitation to the World Series, sitting

Not bad with the glove, either. Maris backs to the seats in
right field, drawing a bead on ball hit by Ken Hunt of
Los Angeles on June 12, 1961, and jackknifes over the low
wall.

regally behind first base while the hawkeyes of the press counted the refreshments and the comments. Lord Mountbatten, later Grand Admiral of the Fleet and already illustrious cousin to the Prince of Wales, ate six ice cream cones and two bags of peanuts, drank four bottles of soda pop, and rooted for Babe Ruth until he was hoarse. Lady Mountbatten, one of the reigning beauties of the Continent, watched through a tortoise-shell lorgnette and shouted things like "Atta boy, Babe." And when the umpire called a strike on Wally Pipp, Her Ladyship was heard to murmur, "Rotten."

Much of the clamor was carried beyond the ball park itself in ripples, then in waves, by the phenomenal new gadget called the radio, and the voice at the microphone at most of the landmark events belonged to a young concert baritone from Washington, D.C., named Graham McNamee.

He had been born in 1889 in the capital but was raised in the Pacific Northwest because his father was a lawyer for the Union Pacific Railroad. Life was serene enough, but it tended to be complicated by his mother's insistence that he play the piano while the other boys on the block were out playing baseball. McNamee did his duty, then at eighteen went his mother one better: he started to take voice lessons to go with the piano lessons. He finally headed for New York to find fame and fortune, but found neither on the concert stage, although he did well enough in his professional debut at Aeolian Hall in 1921 to draw this comment from the critic of the New York *Sun*:

"He sang with a justness, a care and style."

Later, by the time McNamee was singing 150 times in one recital season, he would evoke notices like this one in the *Times*:

"Anyone who sings the air 'O Ruddier Than the Cherry Tree' from Handel's *Acis and Galatea* with such admirably flexible command over the 'divisions,' with such finished phrasing and such excellent enunciation as McNamee showed, is doing a difficult thing very well indeed."

Now it was 1923 and McNamee was getting hungry to try his excellent enunciation on something more rewarding than "O Ruddier Than the Cherry Tree." So one warm day in May, while the Yankees were trying out their new ball park uptown, he strolled up lower Broadway during the luncheon recess in Federal Court, where he had been serving jury duty. He decided to skip lunch, turned instead into the building at number 195, glanced at the sign that read "Radio Station WEAF," and rode the elevator to the little two-room studio on the fourth floor.

He asked the program director, Sam Ross, if he might spend some time looking around and was allowed to peer over the shoulders of a few of the pioneers of commercial radio. By the time he left to go back to the jury box, he had been hired to join the troupe as a jack-of-all-trades — at thirty dollars a week. Three months later, he sat at ringside while Harry Greb was winning the world middleweight championship from Johnny Wilson, describing it blow-by-blow, elbow-by-elbow, with all the old "finished phrasing" that had drawn compliments on the recital stage.

Then it was September, and one day Sam Ross called him in and rewarded him with another assignment: the 1923 World Series. It was just four months after he had wandered away from the jury room, and now he was positioned behind a saucer-shaped microphone in a seat in the open with no precedents or rules to guide or restrict him, and he was becoming the voice behind one of the great spectacles of the day.

He also was surrounded by the biggest crowds in sporting history and, by telephone lines, to even bigger crowds in the crossroads and cities along the Eastern Seaboard. Stations like WJZ in New York, WMAF in South Dartmouth, Massachusetts, and WCAP in Washington, D.C., the press reported, "will also radiate the contests simultaneously with WEAF, as they will be connected by special land wires to microphones controlled by that station."

McNamee did it all with a cultivated voice and an enthusiastic delivery that extracted adventure from every event. After the National Broadcasting Company

Shoe-on-the-other-foot Department: Frank Robinson
returns the favor with similarly acrobatic catch for Baltimore to rob Roy White of game-winning home run.

was organized in 1926, he became a regular visitor into
the parlors of America and he always opened and closed
his broadcasts with a regular greeting: "Good evening,
ladies and gentlemen of the radio audience" at the start
and, at the close, "Good night, all."

He became a celebrity among celebrities at historic
events, like the national political conventions. And his
mail, which began with 1700 letters after the 1923
Series, grew into an avalanche of 50,000 letters after
the 1925 Series.

"You must make each of your listeners, though miles
away from the spot," he reflected, "feel that he or she

too is there with you in that press stand, watching the
pop bottles thrown in the air; Gloria Swanson arriving in
her new ermine coat; McGraw in his dugout, apparently
motionless, but giving signals all the time."

McNamee's choicest superlatives, naturally, were
lavished on the ballplayers who rose above the herd
like the Colossus of Rhodes and, when Ruth went to bat
at a critical point against the Giants, the announcer
even years later described it all in full-bodied prose:

"Then came the thrill of all time, all World Series,
and all sports. Babe Ruth stepped up to bat. One hit
would mean victory for the Yanks, and for them the

Series. It was another Casey at the Bat, and the stands rocked with terrific excitement. John McGraw took the biggest chance of his historic life. He ordered Ryan to pitch to Ruth. The crowd faded into a blurred background. Cheering became silence. Ruth lashed out at the first ball. Ruth hurled his bat and weight against the second. Ruth spun at the third."

That is to say, Ruth struck out. But even when striking out, he became the picture that spoke a thousand words, the man — the *Times* said — who "showed that the Giant supremacy could be broken down. Leading the way himself, he showed that the Giants were not

invincible, that their pitchers could be hit, and that John J. McGraw's strategy, while superb, was not invincible."

"The Ruth," wrote Heywood Broun, "is mighty and shall prevail."

The Ruth was mightiest in 1927, when he cleared sixty fences in the greatest one-man home-run barrage in baseball history. Twenty-eight were hit in Yankee Stadium, thirty-two on the road; the first on April 15 in the stadium off Howard Ehmke of Philadelphia, who had been the victim of that first shot in the park in 1923 while pitching for Boston, and the last on Septem-

In his 2000th game in pinstripes, Yogi Berra pinch-hits a three-run home run on June 9, 1962, and gets the glad hand from Frank Crosetti, senior man on the premises.

ber 30 in the stadium off Tom Zachary of Washington.

There was nothing mathematically magic about the number sixty, not in the sense that other numbers mark the sound barrier at sea level, the force of gravity, or the escape speed from the earth's gravitational pull. But there was something emotionally magic about it. Ruth had hit fifty-nine home runs in 1921, his second season in New York, and had hit as many as forty-seven in 1926. It was intriguing to most people that a man swinging a bat at a baseball thrown from sixty and a half feet away in 154 nine-inning games might reasonably be expected to hit x number of them over a fence. Or, if he were Babe Ruth, then he might outrageously be expected to hit $x + y$ over a fence.

"Ruth's homer," reported James S. Carolan in the *New York Times*, "was a fitting climax to a game that will go down as the Babe's personal triumph. The Yanks scored four runs, the Babe personally crossing the plate three times and bringing in Mark Koenig for the fourth. So this is one time where it would be fair, although not original, to record Yankee victory 109 as Ruth 4, Senators 2.

"There was not much else to the game. The 10,000 persons who came to the Yankee Stadium were there for no other purpose than to see the Babe make home-run history. After each of his visits to the plate, the expectant crowd would relax and wait for his next effort.

"When the Babe stepped to the plate in that momentous eighth inning, the score was deadlocked; Koenig was on third base, the results of a triple; one man was out, and all was tense. It was the Babe's fourth trip to the plate during the afternoon, a base on balls and two singles resulting on his other visits.

"The first Zachary offering was a fast one for a called strike. The next was high. The Babe took a vicious swing at the third pitched ball and the bat connected with a crash that was audible in all parts of the stand. It was not necessary to follow the course of the ball. The boys in the bleachers indicated the route of the record homer. It dropped about halfway to the top.

Autumnal equinox: the name of this game is football.

In the early struggles, Fordham and Pitt would knock heads every year and wind up in a scoreless tie.

Boys, No. 60 was some homer, a fitting wallop to top the Babe's record of 59 in 1921.

"While the crowd cheered and the Yankee players roared their greetings, the Babe made his triumphant, almost regal, tour of the paths. He jogged around slowly, touched each bag firmly and carefully, and when he embedded his spikes in the rubber disk to record officially Homer 60, hats were tossed into the air, papers were torn up and thrown liberally and the spirit of celebration permeated the place.

"The Babe's stroll out to his position was the signal for a handkerchief salute in which all the bleacherites, to the last man, participated. Jovial Babe entered

into the carnival spirit and punctuated his strides with a succession of snappy salutes."

The outpouring of cheers, to say nothing of lush language, reached a peak in the next few days and months and never quite subsided wherever the essential art of a baseball game was celebrated — hitting a ball with a bat. John Kieran took up the chant within twenty-four hours in both prose and poetry.

"It takes quite a bit of remembering to recall that the great home-run hitter was once the best left-handed pitcher in baseball," Kieran wrote. "When he was a member of the Boston Red Sox team, he set a record of pitching twenty-nine scoreless innings in World

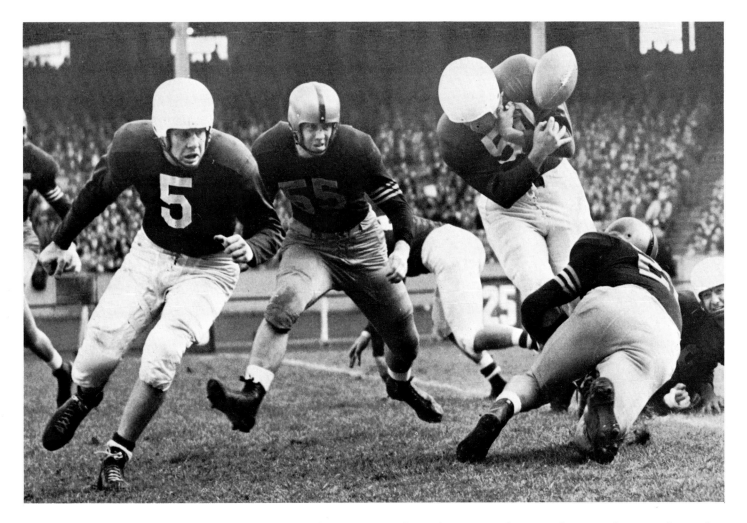

Series competition. Then he started to slip and everybody said the usual thing: 'Good-by Forever' (copyright by Tosti). Babe gathered in all the 'Good-byes' and said: 'Hello, everybody, I'm a heavy-hitting outfielder.'

"And he was. He set a league record of twenty-nine home runs in 1919 and then he came to New York and took the cover off the siege gun.

"That was Ruth's first comeback. A mild one. Others had done that, and the Babe yearned to be distinguished even from a chosen few. He wanted to be the One and Only. He nearly knocked the American League apart with fifty-four home runs in 1920, and in 1921 he set the record at fifty-nine circuit clouts for the season.

"For five years the record was safe enough. In his bland and childlike way, the Babe fell afoul of disciplinary and dietary laws, with the result that he was barred from the diamond for lengthy stretches on orders from Judge Landis, Miller Huggins and the Ruth family physician.

"He set the record of fifty-nine home runs when he was twenty-seven years old. In the following years, he failed to come within hailing distance of his high-water mark, and once again everybody said 'Good-by Forever' (copyright by Tosti).

"Supposedly over the hill, slipping down the steps of Time, stumbling toward the discard, six years past his

69

Army trying to shoot down Michigan pass.

But the long-running show was Army–Notre Dame, a touch of Americana portrayed in programs by Harry Stevens, caterer to the sports world.

peak, Babe Ruth stepped out and hung up a new home-run record at which all the sport world may stand and wonder. What Dempsey did with his fists, Ruth has done with his bat. He came back."

Then, lest the point be lost, Kieran — the columnist, nature expert, bird fancier, and later one of the regular brains of the radio quiz "Information Please" — broke into meter:

ARMY ★ NOTRE DAME ★ 1946

> From "One Old Cat" to the last "At Bat," was
>   there ever a guy like Ruth?
> He can start and go, he can catch and throw, he
>   can field with the very best.
> He's the Prince of Ash and the King of Crash,
>   and that's not an idle jest.
> He can hit that ball o'er the garden wall, high up
>   and far away.
> Beyond the aftermost picket lines where the fleet-
>   footed fielders stray.
> He's the Bogey Man of the pitching clan and he
>   clubs 'em soon and late;
> He has manned his guns and hit home runs from
>   here to the Golden Gate;
> With vim and verve he has walloped the curve
>   from Texas to Duluth,
> Which is no small task, and I beg to ask: Was
>   there ever a guy like Ruth?

Not only was there never a guy like Ruth, but nobody even came close, unless it was the man who batted behind him in the Yankee line-up, "Columbia's ace pitcher" of 1923 — Lou Gehrig. He was a square, stocky giant of a man with the dimpled good looks of an Eagle scout, and he did not have to spend too many afternoons playing baseball on quiet campuses while the Yankees were rocking the rafters crosstown.

Gehrig was sighted, tracked, and appreciated especially by Paul Krichell, the superspy of the Yankees, who watched him play the outfield for Columbia against Rutgers one afternoon in June 1923. Krichell went straight back to New York and told Barrow, in uncommonly extravagant words: "I think I saw another Ruth

Against the Air Force Academy, the cadets march . . .

today." Barrow sent him back for another look and, a few days later, Krichell watched Gehrig hit a ball against the University of Pennsylvania — out of South Field, over the 116th Street walkway, and onto the steps of the Low Memorial Library. The next day, Krichell went back to report again to Barrow, and this time brought an eyewitness with him, Andy Coakley, the Columbia coach.

Before the month was out, Gehrig was headed for the Yankee farm at Hartford, Connecticut, and before September was out he was headed for New York because Wally Pipp had broken several ribs. The Yankees were gliding home in first place by fourteen games, but they needed help in Pipp's absence, so Gehrig made the move from campus to Connecticut to the big stadium, batted .423 in thirteen games, then touched off a tempest in a teapot when the Yankees asked permission to include him on their World Series list of eligibles.

The rub was that no player acquired after September 1 was eligible, though Landis said he would waive the rule if McGraw consented. "The rule is there," McGraw replied, rigid in the face of the enemy, "and if the Yankees have an injury to a regular, it's their hard luck." So the Yankee trainer, Doc Woods, trussed up Pipp, who enjoyed a fine Series while the Yankees finally toppled the Giants from the pinnacle they had perched on for twenty years.

A year and a half later, Gehrig replaced Pipp again at first base, and no understudy ever did it with more finality. The date was June 1, 1925, and he was still there 2130 games later through April 30, 1939, when the undiagnosed early signs of lateral sclerosis were beginning to undermine his immovably strong body. Thirteen full seasons, and most of them spent as the second half of the greatest one-two punch in the business.

Between them, Ruth and Gehrig made the "lively ball" a frightening weapon, forcing pitchers to confront one or the other — or face the alternately revolting danger of putting men on base with the rest of the head-knockers to follow: Meusel, Dugan, Earle Combs, Tony Lazzeri, Bill Dickey, Ben Chapman, and all the rest Barrow had nudged toward New York.

By the time they had stopped — Ruth in 1935 and Gehrig in 1939 — they had belted more baseballs over more obstacles than any pair in history and they had

73

. . . and the cadets ride . . .

revolutionized the game. Ruth ended with 714 home runs, Gehrig with 493, a two-man total of 1207. In thirteen seasons, Ruth hit thirty or more; in seven, he hit forty or more; in four, fifty or more. And the year he hit sixty, Gehrig was connecting with forty-seven and was leading both leagues with 175 runs batted in. Between them, they led the American League thirteen times and in 1925, when they didn't, Meusel set the pace with thirty-three.

When it came to virtuoso performance, they were even more striking. Twenty-three times, Gehrig went the distance with the bases loaded. Twice, Ruth went the distance with the bases loaded in consecutive games. Once, on June 3, 1932, Gehrig hit four home runs in a game and three other times he hit three, while Ruth hit three on two occasions — including May 25, 1935, when he was past forty and playing out his career with the Boston Braves.

They both came to somewhat tragic ends — Gehrig in 1941, his career cut short by muscular disease, and Ruth in 1948, his life cut short by cancer. But they had given the stadium and the game and the public their most melodramatic moments, both in their heyday and in their farewell appearances. And when they were finally gone, after Ruth's death on August 16, 1948, the memories were all over the place.

So was the symbol of a man swiping at a ball. So much so, that Ruth's passing was memorialized in an editorial in the St. Louis *Post-Dispatch* that was titled "Bambino" but that otherwise named no names, simply drawing the portrait of what it all meant in these words:

There he stood, a great tall inverted pyramid at the plate. At the top were two of the broadest, most powerful shoulders the bleachers had ever seen. His slender legs hugged each other and his feet came together like the dot of an exclamation point. He was not fussy. No nervous swinging of the bat. No uneasy kicking of his shoes. No bending over. No straightening up. Just a deliberate getting set. Maybe a little motion at the wrists — that and a death watch on the man on the mound.

Then the first pitch. Low and outside. Everybody tense

In 1956, the stadium becomes the home of the football Giants after thirty seasons in the Polo Grounds, and yard lines replace base lines every autumn.

except the inverted pyramid. Another pitch — low and away. Were they going to walk him? With two on and the winning run at bat, a walk was the play. Then a third pitch. The pyramid gathers himself, steps into the ball and swings — all in one motion. Before the crack of the bat reaches ears in the stands, the ball is lofting away on wings. It rises right of second, arches higher and higher over right field and drops into a sea of upraised hands for another home run. The Babe is jogging around the bags, two runs scoring ahead of him.

Another game won for the New York Yankees, another game nearer the American League pennant and still another World Series. Jogging on, around second, up to third as the din rises, now spikes down on the plate and home again — home for all time.

I saw Yankee Stadium for the first time in September 1928," Joe Cronin remembered, forty-five years later when he was president of the American League. "I'd been called up by Washington in July, but this was our first swing into New York. It was a tourist place, the ball park. Friends of mine from San Francisco came to New York that year and went to see the Statue of Liberty and Yankee Stadium — the Empire State Building wasn't up yet.

"My first day there, I went six-for-eight with two triples during a double-header. I can still hear Miller Huggins in his squeaky voice yelling from the Yankee dugout, 'Curve him, curve him.'

"Once during the afternoon, Bob Meusel got to second base and the Yankee hitter was Leo Durocher. Our pitcher was Fred Marberry and I was playing shortstop. Marberry got behind Durocher and I ran in and said, 'Don't walk this guy, you'll have to pitch to a pinch hitter for the pitcher, and I'd rather have you pitch to this one.' When I went back to my position, Meusel whispered to me, 'You're right, that guy couldn't hit me if I walked in front of the plate.' I remember it so well because they never spoke to the other team then, especially to rookies like me.

Neither snow nor rain nor gloom of night . . .

As Vince Lombardi often said, football is a contact sport.

"I can remember Clark Griffith later, when I was managing Washington — five years later in nineteen thirty-three. I was twenty-seven then but was managing my first club. He would accompany us to New York and sit in a box seat behind the dugout and yell at Babe Ruth. He used to nod toward the stadium in those days and say to me: 'You win or lose it all right here.'"

The year Joe Cronin got his first look at the "'tourist place," the Yankees enlarged the left-field grandstand, adding a mezzanine and upper level so that three decks now stretched around behind home plate and down the foul line. Nine years later, in 1937, they did the same down the right-field line. But the most significant arrivals during those years were three men named Joe — McCarthy, DiMaggio, Louis.

McCarthy was a 5-foot-8-inch Philadelphian with an inexpressive manner and conservative outlook, the master of the noncommittal reply and the devotee of the "set" line-up. He had neither the quiet desperation of Huggins, who preceded him, nor the loud flamboyance of Stengel, who later succeeded both. To some people he was "a push-button manager." To Edward Barrow, who hired him in 1931, he was "the greatest manager who ever lived."

Whatever he was, Joseph Vincent McCarthy joined the team after it had won six pennants and three World Series under Huggins in the nineteen twenties and, for the next fifteen seasons, he called the shots for them through a Depression and World War — adding eight pennants and seven world titles.

He had never played an inning of major-league baseball, but had spent twenty years as a player and manager in the minors before William Wrigley hired him as manager of the Chicago Cubs in 1926. Three years later, they won the National League pennant, and two years after that, McCarthy switched to the rival league and the Yankees.

By 1931, the Yankees were still the toast of the town, but they were aging somewhat as they turned into the

Bodies strewn all over the stadium grass, and Leroy Kelly of the Cleveland Browns winds up in the arms of a defensive pincers by the Giants.

The big rush in the mud, but the punt gets launched
anyway.

TOUCHDOWN!

new decade and for three years running had finished second or third while Connie Mack's Philadelphia Athletics outgalloped the field. One year after he took charge, though, the Yankees won 107 games and the pennant with newcomers like Frank Crosetti, Bill Dickey, Lefty Gomez, and Red Ruffing joining the only holdovers from the Huggins era — Ruth, Gehrig, and Lazzeri.

In four games that fall in the 1932 Series, the Yankees not only outshouted the Cubs in dugout repartee but flattened them for the title while Ruth "called" his legendary shot before hitting a titanic home run off Charlie Root in Wrigley Field. It marked a sort of sweet revenge for McCarthy, who had been more or less drummed out of Chicago after Philadelphia had scored ten runs in one inning against his Cubs in the 1929 Series. And it also marked the final flourish of the older Yankees who had opened the stadium ten seasons earlier.

Three years in second place followed, though, as the country spiraled downward into the Depression and attendance at the ball park dwindled to 728,014 in 1933, a loss of nearly 50 per cent since the glamour days. The hard times were occasionally relieved by mayors like Fiorello H. La Guardia, who would throw out the first ball of the season with the same runaway zest he showed while reading the comics on the radio — under a home-team baseball cap, from the pitcher's mound, with full wind-up.

But a more enduring relief was being concocted by Barrow and his new farm director, George Weiss, an organizer and impresario from New Haven who began gathering one of the most fruitful minor-league systems in the business. And as he did, scouts like Joe Devine and Bill Essick prowled the landscape lining up talent and offering the country boys one-way tickets to Yankee Stadium.

One of the tickets was handed, in 1936, to a twenty-one-year-old San Franciscan named Joseph Paul Di-Maggio and, with him forming the last link from Ruth

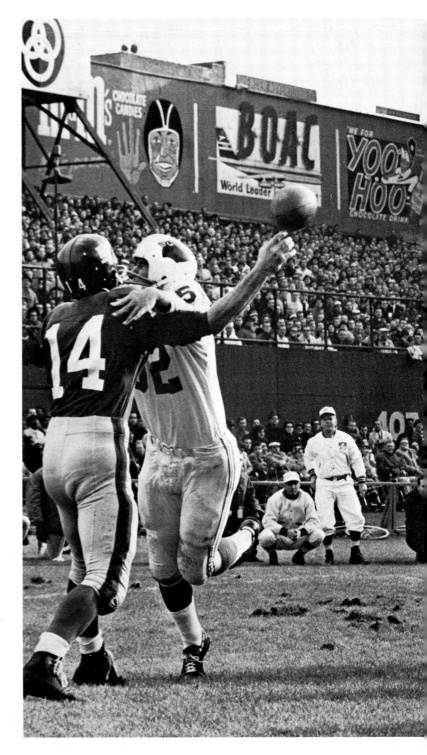

December 28, 1958: The Baltimore Colts and the New York Giants meet in the stadium for the championship of the National Football League, and before the afternoon is over, people will be calling it "the greatest football game ever played."

One reason it was such a great game was John Unitas, the Colts quarterback; another was the defense the Giants aimed at him.

to Gehrig and beyond, the team struck that season with blitzkrieg force — and kept striking for the next four seasons.

In 1936, they won 102 games, lost 51, and defeated the Giants in six games in the Series. In 1937, they won 102, lost 52, and took the Giants in five. In 1938, they won 99, lost 53, and swept the Cubs again in four. And in 1939, they won 106, lost 45, and swept the Cincinnati Reds.

By now, Gehrig had left the club at his own insistence, and he had left the scene without self-pity, declaring at a poignant farewell appearance that summer that he considered himself "the luckiest man on the face of the earth." The club, meanwhile, absorbed the loss of both Gehrig and Ruth and kept rolling along while Weiss kept channeling new players into the mainstream — Phil Rizzuto, Spud Chandler, Tiny Bonham, Joe Gordon, Tommy Henrich, and legions of others who often simply crossed the country from farm teams at Kansas City, or the Hudson River from Newark, and set up shop in the Bronx.

The people kept coming, too. For one double-header between the Yankees and Boston Red Sox on May 30, 1938, the turnstiles clicked 81,841 times. For one football game twenty years later, *the* game between the New York Giants and Baltimore Colts, the crowd reached 71,163. And for the heavyweight title fight on June 12, 1930, between Max Schmeling and Jack Sharkey: 79,222.

Sometimes, the final touch of stadium history was applied someplace else, as it was on the night of July 17, 1941, when 67,466 fans paid their way into Cleveland's Municipal Stadium. The advertised occasion was a baseball game between the Yankees and Indians, and the Yankees won it, 4 to 3. But the real lure was Di-Maggio, who was greeted with stormy applause every time he went to the plate — four times, to be exact. He had hit safely in fifty-six games in a row since May 15 against the Chicago White Sox, he already had crashed his way through both the American and Na-

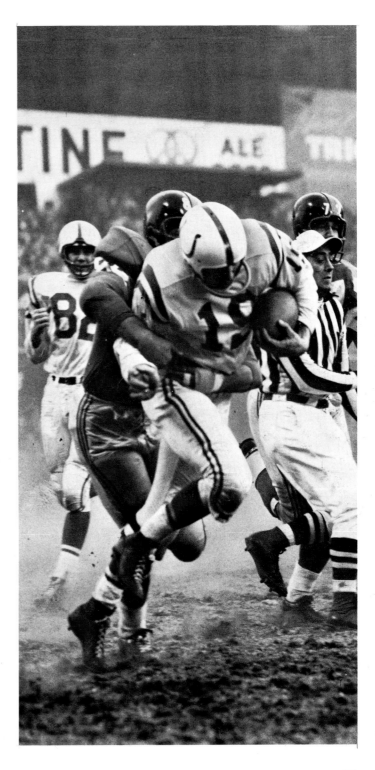

With seven seconds to go, Steve Myhra kicks a 20-yard field goal to tie the score at 17-17 and send them into sudden-death overtime . . .

tional League records for consistent hitting, and he even had hit safely in the All-Star Game nine days earlier.

During his two-month siege, the twenty-six-year-old "Yankee Clipper" had taken his long-legged stride to the plate 223 times, had made 91 hits that included 15 home runs, and had scored 56 times — once a game. Four times, he made four hits in a game; five times, he got three; and thirteen times, two. He averaged .408 in that stretch, and the whole country began to follow his trips to bat as the streak grew.

On June 29, in a double-header in Washington, he tied the American League record of forty-one games set by George Sisler of the St. Louis Browns nineteen years earlier; in the second game, he broke it. On July 1, he tied the all-time record of forty-four games set by Willie Keeler, the old cue shark of the Baltimore Orioles, and the following day he broke that one. Then, with that particular pressure off, he got twenty-three hits in his next forty times up, and he had

a fifty-six-game streak going the night he faced the Indians in Cleveland.

Three times that night, DiMaggio swung against the veteran left-hander Al Smith. Twice he smashed the ball down the third-base line, and twice Ken Keltner made remarkable stops to throw him out. In between, he drew a base on balls, and then in the eighth inning he swung against the young right-hander Jim Bagby with the bases loaded and one down. On the one-ball, one-strike pitch, he unloaded his third shot of the night, another rocket, but straight at the shortstop Lou Boudreau, who collared it, threw to Ray Mack for one out, and on to Oscar Grimes for the double play.

The Yankees, who had had a streak of their own broken the year before after four world championships in a row, got their second wind during DiMaggio's streak that summer and streaked to another pennant. They then overpowered the revived Brooklyn Dodgers in five games in the Series, giving McCarthy his sixth title and breaking the record of his hometown hero,

. . . and sudden death comes when Alan Ameche storms across the Giants' goal line while Unitas leans and Lenny Moore blocks.

Tittle stands at attention in the dugout for the National Anthem on December 12, 1964 — his last day in uniform number 14 — and later sits and reflects, a man with his memories.

Connie Mack. They took the pennant again the next year, 1942, but finally lost the Series in five games to the St. Louis Cardinals—a Series that McCarthy opened with the battery from the 1932 Series: Ruffing and Dickey.

Then, in 1943, with DiMaggio and many of the others in military service, McCarthy pieced together his last winner. Nick Etten was at first base now, Billy Johnson at third, Johnny Lindell in center in place of Number Five, and the long-time relief specialist Johnny Murphy in the bullpen. In the Series, they took the Cardinals in five games for McCarthy's seventh

world title in eight tries, awakening the catchword of the late thirties, "Break up the Yankees."

To which McCarthy replied, when people questioned his contribution to all this maurauding: "Sure, I spend every summer in Atlantic City and only come back to get ready for the World Series."

Three years later, unsettled by a stomach ailment and by the flamboyant style of the Yankees' new president, Larry MacPhail, the man they called "Marse Joe" quit while Dickey and then Bucky Harris took over the "push-button" ball club.

They had given baseball something that was mono-

88

lithic, and they had done it with muscle and with straight, sound, and unspectacular strategy. They were men, but they bulldozed the landscape like machines. And their relentless, impersonal manner was typified one day by an incident outside the Chase Hotel in St. Louis, where Dickey was accosted by a former Philadelphia player, Joe Gantenbein.

"Hey, Bill, do you remember me?" Gantenbein asked.

Dickey looked him over in the best Yankee manner and replied from cold memory: "I'm sorry. I can't remember your name. But I know we used to pitch you high and outside."

June 19, 1936: The ring had been built near second base in the infield where the Yankee "machine" was starting its right-on roll. DiMaggio, pokerfaced, was a rookie establishing his beachhead in the stadium. But on this night, the home team was traveling, and its place in center stage was taken by another pokerfaced Joe — Joe Louis Barrow, the baby heavyweight from Alabama and Detroit. He was an 8 to 1 favorite that night to extend his string of knockouts against the field, twenty-three knockouts in twenty-seven victories in a row, and his "victim" was the ex-champion, Max Schmeling of Germany, predicting that beyond the business at hand he would become the first fighter to *regain* the heavyweight title.

Joe Louis shuffles in, his hands set dead ahead, his head slightly dipped, his expression impassive, oblivious to Schmeling's prefight trumpeting that he had "seen something" revealing in the films of Louis's earlier bouts. He shuffles ahead and suddenly, in the fourth round, Schmeling unfurls a long right hand to the left temple and Louis hits the deck. He bounces back up at the count of two and is hit by more right hands as he tries to land his left-right combinations, the fastest in the business. They keep fighting as the noise drowns out the bell and, as round five ends, Louis catches a whistling right flush on the jaw and barely makes it back to his corner.

By the twelfth round, Jack Blackburn has run out of his urgent whisperings and Louis has run out of strength. He strikes back, almost from memory, but for the second time in the ordeal he hits below the belt and draws a warning from the referee, Arthur Donovan. And Schmeling, though hurt in the exchanges, explodes another right hand to the jaw, another to the face, and another to the blinking, troubled eyes. Then a haymaker to the jaw and, as Donovan tolls the count, the unbeaten Brown Bomber manages to raise his shoulders slightly, gets to one elbow at "seven," and lies helpless among the cobwebs at "ten" and out.

June 22, 1938: They arrive early, the crowd of close to 80,000, paying up to thirty dollars for a seat on the infield grass, judges and senators and representatives and governors, and Jim Farley sitting up close within earshot of the broadcasters describing the scene in English, German, Spanish, and Portuguese. Now Max Schmeling is thirty-two, after fourteen years in the prize ring, trying to accomplish something that was not accomplished by Jim Corbett, Bob Fitzsimmons, Jim Jeffries, and Jack Dempsey — trying to win the heavyweight championship for the second time. It was the one thing he could not accomplish that night two years earlier, but since then the title has been won by Joe Louis, who has won thirty-eight of thirty-nine fights, and the thirty-ninth was the twelve-round battering against Max.

This time, Joe Louis shuffles only briefly, then starts stalking. He flicks both hands toward Schmeling, then rips both hands at the German, who sinks unbelieving for a count of "three." Then he surfaces and is overpowered again, Joe Louis swarming over him along the ropes, and Schmeling falls again. Back up before Arthur Donovan counts past "one," but no reprieve. He is down again under a barrage at pointblank range and, as the count reaches "three," Max Machon flutters a white towel through the ropes into the ring, hoisting the European signal for "S.O.S." and "We surrender" all at once. Donovan, in the American manner, gathers it

91

up and flings it back through the ropes, returns to Schmeling's crumpled figure, quits counting at "five," and spreads both hands out flat, palms down.

It is two years later. Two years, two minutes, and four seconds later.

"When I was a kid, which was before Joe Louis became the champion, I used to take the train from my home in Alabama, where Joe came from, and go to Detroit, where he lived," Mel Allen remembered. "It was summertime, and I'd stay with my aunt.

"Once I went out to Navin Field, where the Tigers played, and saw Babe Ruth catch a fly ball for the final out in the last half of the eighth inning. The Tigers were ahead of the Yankees by five runs and, after Ruth caught the ball, he trotted in past the Tigers dugout and then decided to sit in it during the top of the ninth. He wasn't supposed to come up to bat anyway, and the umpires didn't say anything — he was Babe Ruth.

"But, as luck would have it, the Yankees started to rally and after a while it was his turn to bat. So he crossed the field to the Yankee side, picked out his bat, and — so help me — hit a home run over the center-field fence with two men on base, and the Yankees ended up with six runs and the game."

The story seemed as improbable as Melvin Allen Israel, the oldest of three children born to Julius and Anna Israel, both natives of Russia. They lived in Johns, outside Birmingham, where the father owned a general store and where Mel grew up tall and smart and precocious. He graduated from grammar school at eleven, from high school at fifteen; he played football, baseball, and basketball in high school; he worked for a time as a batboy in North Carolina in the Piedmont League; and he even sold soda pop in the Detroit ball park, where Babe Ruth could turn in a flash from fraternizing to outright aggression.

He enrolled at the University of Alabama in 1928, majored in political science, got his Bachelor of Arts in 1932, entered law school, and completed a law degree in 1936. However, he had won a fellowship as a speech

LEFT AND BELOW June 22, 1938: Joe Lewis avenges his
defeat — two years, two minutes, and four seconds later.

93

Louis mixes it with Billy Conn, one of his most warlike opponents in a long and dramatic career.

Championship Fights at Yankee Stadium

July 24, 1923	Leonard vs. Tendler	15 rounds
June 26, 1924	Greb vs. Moore	15
May 30, 1925	Berlenbach vs. McTigue	15
Sept. 11, 1925	Berlenbach vs. Slattery	11 (KO)
Sept. 25, 1925	Walker vs. Slade	15
June 10, 1926	Berlenbach vs. Stribling	15
June 26, 1928	Tunney vs. Heeney	11 (KO)
July 18, 1929	Loughran vs. Braddock	15
June 12, 1930	Schmeling vs. Sharkey	4 (foul)
July 17, 1930	Singer vs. Mandell	1 (KO)
Aug. 30, 1937	Louis vs. Farr	15
June 22, 1938	Louis vs. Schmeling	1 (KO)
June 20, 1939	Louis vs. Galento	4 (KO)
Aug. 22, 1939	Ambers vs. Armstrong	15
June 28, 1940	Louis vs. Godoy	8 (KO)
June 19, 1946	Louis vs. Conn	8 (KO)
Sept. 18, 1946	Louis vs. Mauriello	1 (KO)
Sept. 27, 1946	Zale vs. Graziano	6 (KO)
June 25, 1948	Louis vs. Walcott	11 (KO)
Sept. 23, 1948	Williams vs. Flores	10 (KO)
Aug. 10, 1949	Charles vs. Lesnevich	7 (KO)
June 27, 1950	Charles vs. Louis	15
Sept. 8, 1950	Saddler vs. Pep	8 (KO)
June 25, 1952	Maxim vs. Robinson	14 (KO)
June 17, 1954	Marciano vs. Charles	15
Sept. 17, 1954	Marciano vs. Charles	8 (KO)
Sept. 21, 1955	Marciano vs. Moore	9 (KO)
Sept. 23, 1957	Basilio vs. Robinson	15
June 26, 1959	Johansson vs. Patterson	3 (KO)

A "national resource" of Brazil at work
— Edson Arantes do Nascimento, the one and only Pele, the
one-time shoeshine boy who scored more than 1000 goals
in fourteen seasons as the premier soccer star in the world.

instructor and before long literally talked himself out of his long-time ambition of becoming a lawyer.

The switch came when Frank Thomas, the football coach, asked him to handle the public-address broadcasts at home games. Then he started to announce sports for a local radio station and finally Ted Husing put him on the air between halves of the Alabama-Tulane game. Next he was headed for an audition at the Columbia Broadcasting System in New York.

"I told them I wasn't really interested," he recalled, thirty-five years later, drinking a carton of milk from the roof of a rented car in the parking lot at Huggins-Stengel Field in St. Petersburg, Florida. "I wanted to go home and start practicing law. But I remembered some wild rumors about those auditions — they were supposed to put you into a room with no windows and make you ad-lib for thirty minutes or something.

"So I decided to find out, and what I found out was that it was no such thing. They gave me things to read, like a symphony program to see if I could get the composers' names right, and a commercial and things like that. On New Year's Eve, I was on my way out when I got a telegram saying I'd got the job. I still wasn't convinced, but they let me go back to school and give the final semester exams, and I told the president of the university I'd be leaving in four months anyway. Then I went back to New York and became a staff announcer at forty-five a week.

"After a while, I landed an extra job as the announcer on the 'Pick and Pat Show' and got the munificent sum of fifty dollars extra for that. But that was good money in those days. I also was named the back-up man to Bob Trout on special events and Ted Husing in sports, both tops in their field, and one night I was sent into

People, politicians, Presidents, preachers, Popes all
appeared on the stadium stage during its first half-century.
Fiorello H. La Guardia, a method actor, opens the season
for the Yankees in 1934 by burning a mayoral fast ball over
the plate.

the little news booth to read a bulletin — interrupting the 'Kate Smith Hour' to read that the *Hindenburg* had burned and crashed at Lakehurst, New Jersey."

He had the gift of gab, all right, a southern accent surrounded by pearl-shaped tones and perfect enunciation, and in 1938 they were all put to work on color commentary at the World Series — fifteen years after Graham McNamee's "excellent enunciation" had been put to work over WEAF. One season later, CBS began broadcasting the home games of the Yankees and Giants, and the former speech teacher from Alabama became the number two man to Arch McDonald. And when McDonald left in 1940, the soft southern accent became the number one voice describing the adventures of the New York Yankees for the next twenty-four seasons.

At his peak, he received a thousand letters a week, a couple of hundred thousand dollars a year, and one flower a day from an anonymous lady admirer. In a typical week, he might broadcast eight Yankee games in three cities, play in two or three charity softball games in three states, record two Movietone newsreels, and then maybe head for the All-Star baseball game.

But his home base remained the stadium, and his household terms referred to the ball club that lived there. He characterized ballplayers as folk heroes, making "Yankee Clipper" synonymous with DiMaggio and "The Scooter" with Phil Rizzuto, and reflecting astonishment at their exploits with a soaring exclamation: "How about that!" He acknowledged that he was "partisan," but denied that he was "prejudiced," and insisted that "I always make a point of giving the other teams their due."

By the time he had left the scene, he had broadcast almost 4000 baseball games on radio and television, including six no-hitters, and along the way he also described twenty World Series, a dozen Rose Bowl games in California, and numerous horse races, basketball double-headers, and regattas. When he arrived in 1939, the Yankees were becoming the dominant power in baseball; when he announced his last game

... and Edward G. Barrow, who had helped Ruppert start
the dynasty two generations earlier ...

in 1964, the empire was under great pressure. But for all the seasons in between, from Lou Gehrig to Joe DiMaggio to Casey Stengel to Mickey Mantle, he was the man at the microphone and the voice of the Yankees.

As such, he also became the master of ceremonies whenever Fiorello H. La Guardia would fire the first ball from the pitcher's mound or whenever the borough president appeared bearing citations or whenever the club or the fans joined the trend toward bestowing a "day" on a player. He also was with the team as a rookie broadcaster in 1939 when Gehrig stalked McCarthy as the manager stepped out of an elevator at the Book-Cadillac Hotel in Detroit, walked over, and said: "You'd better take me out today, Joe."

McCarthy, sensing the anguish behind the remark, decided on the spot not to fuss. "Whatever you say, Lou," he replied, nodding a little remotely. "It's up to you."

"I decided on it Sunday night," Gehrig explained later, just before the Yankees took the field without him for the first time since 1925. "I knew after Sunday's game that I ought to get out of there. I got up four times with men on base. Once there were two on. A hit any of those times would have won the game. But I left all five men on."

As the team's captain, Gehrig did carry the line-up card to home plate and handed it to the umpire in chief. Then he made the strange journey to the dugout and sat on the bench, while other men stared straight ahead pretending not to notice and Lefty Gomez gave it the old college try. "Hell, Lou," he quipped to no particular laughter, "it took them fifteen years to get you out of the ball game. Sometimes they get me out of there in fifteen minutes."

A month later, Gehrig left the Mayo Clinic carrying a sealed envelope containing X-ray pictures and a diagnosis of his condition. The diagnosis, which he released to the public, read:

"He is suffering from amyotrophic lateral sclerosis. This type of illness involves the motor pathways and cells of the central nervous system, and in lay terms is

. . . and James Lyons, Borough President of the Bronx,
who gave it the modified City Hall treatment . . .

known as a form of chronic poliomyelitis (infantile
paralysis). The nature of this trouble makes it such
that Mr. Gehrig will be unable to continue his active
participation as a baseball player."

Eight years later, after the cheers and tears for Gehrig
had subsided, a sellout crowd packed the park on Sunday, April 27, 1947. They called it Babe Ruth Day,
though it really marked phase two of the passing of the
guard. Ruth, fatally ill with cancer, made it up the
dugout steps with a boost while the crowd rose and
roared — a stooped and wasted figure in the old camel's
hair coat and cap. He was barely able to acknowledge
the ovation because an operation on his throat had left
his voice hoarse, but he made a little speech of thanks
and observed that "the only real game, I think, in the
world, is baseball."

He turned around, unsteady, and groped toward the
dugout while the next generation of ballplayers, including Yogi Berra, struggled with the urge to lend a
hand. Then they watched while Cardinal Spellman, the
Archbishop of New York, shook his hand and said,
"Good luck, Babe."

"I just wanted to say," the cardinal added, "that
any time you want me to come to your home and give
you Holy Communion, I'll be glad to do it."

Ruth acknowledged the offer with a grin and replied:
"Thanks, Your Eminence. Thanks just the same, but
I'd rather come down to your place."

The first time I saw the stadium was in August of
nineteen forty-three," Danny Murtaugh was saying,
almost twenty years later. "I had just been inducted
into the army and they took me out of Fort Meade,
Maryland, because I was a ballplayer. We were an
army team and were brought to New York to play
against a combined Dodger–Giant–Yankee team. The
idea was to raise money for war bonds.

"The game itself was in the Polo Grounds, but we
worked out in Yankee Stadium, and that was my first

The first-ball renaissance gets a hand from Paul Simon on an afternoon when Simon and Garfunkel put baseball ahead of music. This time, William Paley of CBS monitors the left-handed pitch.

RIGHT Mrs. Babe Ruth, a frequent visitor to a house of memories . . .

look. I was awed. It wasn't any bigger than the other ball parks, but it had a history that was bigger. Ruth, Gehrig, the whole thing.

"We did okay on the war bonds. They sold several hundred million dollars' worth, and my wife came up from Chester, Pennsylvania, and sat in a box seat that was auctioned off for ten thousand dollars. They were selling them off to the highest bidders, and the money went into the bonds.

"The next time I saw the stadium was in nineteen sixty, seventeen years later. It was the World Series, and I was managing 'the other team' — the Pittsburgh Pirates — against the Yankees. By then I wasn't so awed anymore, I'd been around long enough not to be awed, and we had plenty of work to do. But the memories were still there . . ."

Between Danny Murtaugh's two visits to the Bronx, a lot of "new" memories were cranked into the Yankees ball yard by people named Rocky Marciano, Andy Robustelli, Floyd Patterson, Sam Huff, Sugar Ray Robinson, Robert F. Wagner, John Unitas, Francis Cardinal Spellman, and a baldish, oldish right-handed passer called Y. A. Tittle. To say nothing of Steve Owen,

Mickey Mantle, Frank Gifford, Elston Howard, Carmen Basilio, Kyle Rote, Billy Graham, Roosevelt Grier, Ingemar Johansson, Charley Conerly, and a fresh-faced left-handed pitcher called Whitey Ford.

But much of the traffic in the park was directed, and sometimes compounded, by the stumpy, gnarled, bow-legged old outfielder who had hit the first World Series home run there a generation or two earlier, Casey Stengel, though his chief claim to fame by then may have been his landslide election in 1944 as the "funniest" manager in the big leagues. He was bearing down on his fifty-fifth birthday then, and he received four times as many votes in the poll as the runner-up, Jimmy Dykes, and six times as many as the number three man, Charlie Grimm, who played the banjo and was considered exceptionally funny, even by Stengel.

Consequently, it came as a distinct shock to most persons when Stengel surfaced suddenly in New York in October 1948 and was introduced as the next manager of the New York Yankees, the most exceedingly unfunny — and consistently successful — baseball team in history. His accession was widely regarded as an interim step between dynasties, as when John XXIII was elected Pope a dozen years later and was considered by many persons a "transition Pope." And the results in Stengel's case were almost as surprising.

By then, the Yankees had rolled along to fifteen American League pennants and eleven world championships, principally under Miller Huggins and Joe McCarthy, before adjusting to the leaner days of World War II. They finished third in 1944, then fourth in 1945, edged back to third in 1946, all the way back to first in 1947, but then settled again into third place in 1948 under Stanley (Bucky) Harris, who had been installed by Larry MacPhail. Finally, after a fairly sensational brawl in public, MacPhail had been bought out for $2,000,000 by his partners, Dan Topping and Del Webb, and the Yankees were straining to recapture their serenity in the fall of 1948 when George Weiss ushered in Charles Dillon Stengel.

Casey's gift of gab immediately transformed the

. . . a young Joe DiMaggio watches an old Connie Mack get the municipal handshake and scroll from Mayor William O'Dwyer . . .

. . . and old Casey Stengel stands by while number 5 greets
General Douglas MacArthur and his lady.

mood around the stadium, but for most of the season it competed for attention with his players' physical problems. Joe DiMaggio missed the first sixty-five games because of a bone spur on his heel, then missed two more weeks in September because of a virus infection. Tommy Henrich had a wrenched knee, Charley Keller a chronic back ailment, and Yogi Berra a broken finger. Seven men played first base at one time or another — Henrich, Johnny Mize, Dick Kryhoski, Jack Phillips, Billy Johnson, Fenton Mole, and Joe Collins. Third base was shared by Johnson, a part-time first baseman, and Bobby Brown, a part-time medical student. Two accomplished midgets played shortstop and second base, Phil Rizzuto and George Stirnweiss. They were supported by Jerry Coleman, a Marine Corps Reserve pilot who shuttled between the infield and the Marines for years. Berra, an outfielder, was made a catcher. And Johnny Lindell, a pitcher, was made an outfielder.

Every day when he arrived for work, Stengel would first check with the trainer, Gus Mauch, to determine the able-bodied men before writing nine names on his line-up card in a Victorian script. Things got so bad that he wrote the names of his three middle batters — Henrich, DiMaggio, and Berra — only seventeen times as a unit in 154 games.

"Every time I'd walk into Stengel's office," recalled Mauch, a trim man in white slacks and tennis sneakers who held degrees as a doctor of naturopathy and doctor of chiropractics, "and I'd say, 'Your star outfielder is hurt and can't play.' And he'd say, 'Thank you, doctor.' He never blinked an eye.

"Joe DiMaggio had a pain in his heel like the pain of a hundred carpet tacks," Mauch said. "He had a flock of tiny calcium deposits that had to solidify into one before the pain would stop. We could have filled a Fibber McGee closet with all the contraptions that shoe companies sent us to correct the problem. They sent shoes with half soles in the front and iron bars in the rear, and people who had had bone spurs sent advice and even medicine."

Mel Allen, the voice of the Yankees, gets one trophy and two smiles from Thomas E. Dewey, the voice of New York, and Happy Chandler, the voice of Kentucky who became commissioner.

The sixties scene: Mike Burke welcomes Hubert H. Humphrey, the happy warrior and incorrigible baseball fan . . .

One day DiMaggio stepped out of bed and discovered that the pain in his famous right heel had gone. It was already late in June and the Yankees were struggling to keep pace with the Boston Red Sox of Ted Williams, Bobby Doerr, Dominic DiMaggio, Ellis Kinder, and Mel Parnell, a talented bunch who played for the old Yankee boss, Joe McCarthy. The Yankees had an exhibition game on June 27 against the Giants, and DiMaggio walked into Stengel's office while Casey was fiddling with his line-up card and said, "I think I'll give it a whirl tonight, Case."

He played the whole game and then, the next night in Boston, got back into the regular line-up with a single and home run, added two home runs the next day, and another the day after that, and then wound up on the cover of *Life* magazine as a sort of medical freak. His return triggered a series of switches by Stengel, who pulled substitutes out of his hat as the injuries continued until, on Saturday, October 1, the Yankees returned home one game behind Boston with two games left to play — against Boston. And the *New York Times* paused in its coverage of the world scene to editorialize: "We will not believe that our Casey has struck out until the baseball mathematicians say the Yankees are impossible."

In the home dugout, while 69,551 customers howled in the stands and carloads of gifts were toted onto the grass for Joe DiMaggio Day, the Professor ignored the odds and ventured: "I think we've got 'em. I feel it in my bones."

Nine innings later, after spotting the Red Sox four fast runs, the Yankees pulled it out, 5 to 4, and the next day — the final day — gave it the winner-take-all treatment before 68,055 persons. This time, it was 1 to 0, Yankees, with Vic Raschi pitching, until the last half of the eighth. Then each side fired some late salvos to make the final score 5 to 3, Yankees, and the old man's bones were vindicated.

"We had seventy-two injuries that season," recalled Gus Mauch, whose ribs were taped that fall following a collision with a parking meter on a Boston sidewalk.

... and Senator Eugene McCarthy, the Minnesota colleague of Senator Humphrey and a ballplayer himself.

"I mean, seventy-two injuries that kept a man out of the line-up. And when Henrich caught the foul ball that ended that last game and gave us the pennant, Bill Dickey jumped up in the dugout and cracked his head on the roof. That made seventy-three."

For the next dozen years, Stengel presided over the dugout with nonstop monologues and with practically nonstop success. The Yankees won five straight pennants and World Series, then finished second in 1954, then won five of the next six pennants plus two more Series. Players came and went, but the supply seemed as endless as the dangerous way they lived on the field, and as endless as Stengel's theatrics.

In the spring of 1951, DiMaggio added a bit of urgency to the situation by announcing that he intended to retire after the season. But when the team pitched camp in Arizona that February, all eyes turned to a stocky, brutally strong blond from Oklahoma named Mickey Charles Mantle, a twenty-year-old switch-hitter with speed, power, osteomyelitis in his left ankle, and a 4-F rating in the military draft. He had played professionally at Independence, Kansas, in 1949 and at Joplin, Missouri, in 1950 after Tom Greenwade, the Yankee superscout, had braced him with a $1000 bonus. Stengel stashed him on the farm at Kansas City for forty games, then brought him up to the Yankees for ninety-six. He hit thirteen home runs, stayed for eighteen seasons, and hit 523 more — 373 left-handed, 163 right-handed.

Nine of his home runs were hit with the bases loaded, 18 others were hit in the World Series, 270 were hit on the road, and 266 were hit in Yankee Stadium. Some of them traveled very long distances, regardless of whose tape measure was being used, including three that reached the center-field bleachers in one game against Detroit on May 13, 1955. Twice he reached the façade of the upper deck in right field, bringing him close to the distinction of driving a ball *out* of the park, and one of them — off Bill Fischer of Kansas City on May 22, 1963 — was still rising when it

bounced off the roof's façade, prompting Mantle to rate it "the hardest ball I ever hit."

As the centerpiece — and center fielder — of the Yankees in the line of succession from Ruth to Gehrig to DiMaggio, the Switcher was surrounded by plenty of help.

There was Allie Reynolds, who pitched a no-hit game against Cleveland on July 12, 1951, Mantle's rookie season, and who then pitched another against Boston on September 28. His catcher both times was Berra, the short and blunt folk hero of the club, who was constructed along lines of fireplug simplicity and who sometimes matched Stengel in folk wisdom with lines like: "You can observe a lot just by watching."

On the day that Reynolds pitched his second no-hitter, Yogi gave Stengel and the rest of the Yankees, to say nothing of Reynolds, a moment of runaway excitement. With two outs in the ninth inning and Reynolds one out from baseball history, Ted Williams lifted a towering foul ball off to the side of home plate. Berra circled under the ball, drew a bead on it, tossed his mask out of the way, waited — and dropped the ball. Now Reynolds was still one out from baseball history, but the one out was Williams, a bad man to play games with.

"I called for the same pitch the second time," Berra remembered, reviewing the technicalities of the embarrassing moment. "Fast ball across the letters and tight. And Reynolds pitched it right there."

And, while Stengel and everybody else cringed in wonder, Williams lifted an identical foul ball off to the side of the plate — and this time Yogi squeezed it for the twenty-seventh and last out.

Five years later, on October 8, 1956, Berra was behind the plate on another memorable occasion, with Mantle in center field, Enos Slaughter in left, Hank Bauer in right, an infield of Collins, Billy Martin, Gil McDougald, and Andy Carey — and 64,519 persons in the stands watching a twenty-seven-year-old right-hander named Don Larsen pitching against the Dodg-

Burke, who suggested that the Yankees could use some clout to regain their rank, practices what he preaches.

ers in the World Series. Earlier that year, Larsen had achieved notoriety by running his car into a tree one night in St. Petersburg, Florida, drawing a low-keyed warning from Stengel that the next such incident would involve a stack of money.

But on this day seven months later, Larsen paid Casey back for his forbearance by delivering ninety-six pitches to the Dodgers — number ninety-six being a shoulder-high fast ball that Dale Mitchell, a pinch hitter, looked at and that Babe Pinelli, the home-plate umpire, called strike three. It was the third out of the ninth inning and the twenty-seventh *in a row* of the game for Larsen, completing the first perfect game in Series history. The box score read like this:

BROOKLYN (N.L.)	ab	r	h	o	a		NEW YORK (A.L.)	ab	r	h	o	a
Gilliam, 2b	3	0	0	2	0		Bauer, rf	4	0	1	4	0
Reese, ss	3	0	0	4	2		Collins, 1b	4	0	1	7	0
Snider, cf	3	0	0	1	0		Mantle, cf	3	1	1	4	0
Robinson, 3b	3	0	0	2	4		Berra, c	3	0	0	7	0
Hodges, 1b	3	0	0	5	1		Slaughter, lf	2	0	0	1	0
Amoros, lf	3	0	0	3	0		Martin, 2b	3	0	1	3	4
Furillo, rf	3	0	0	0	0		McDougald, ss	2	0	0	0	2
Campanella, c	3	0	0	7	2		Carey, 3b	3	1	1	1	1
Maglie, p	2	0	0	0	1		Larsen, p	2	0	0	0	1
a-Mitchell	1	0	0	0	0			26	2	5	27	8
Total	27	0	0	24	10							

a- Called out on strikes for Maglie in ninth.

Brooklyn .... 0 0 0 0 0 0 0 0 0 — 0
New York .... 0 0 0 1 0 1 0 0 x — 2

Errors — none. Runs batted in — Mantle, Bauer. Home run — Mantle. Sacrifice — Larsen. Double plays — Reese and Hodges; Hodges, Campanella, Robinson, Campanella and Robinson. Left on base — Dodgers 0, Yankees 3. Bases on balls: Maglie, 2. Struck out — Larsen, 7; Maglie, 5. Umpires — Pinelli (N), Soar (A), Boggess (N), Napp (A), Gorman (N), Runge (A).

Time — 2:06. Attendance — 64,519.

Four years and three pennants later, the Professor was gone from the Yankee Stadium scene, though his imprint and language survived. His imprint included ten league titles and seven world titles in twelve years, as well as a generation of ballplayers like Mantle who, Casey reflected, "thinks I was born at the age of sixty-two and started managing immediately."

Triumvirate of the seventies: Ralph Houk, Lee MacPhail,
Mike Burke.

Pete Sheehy was invited inside in 1927 to help out, and stayed — as master of the clubhouse for generations of Yankees.

RIGHT, TOP   The old-timers might mistake it for the Taj Mahal, but behind the scenes and beneath the stadium, the moderns relax in splendor waiting for the day's adventures . . .
RIGHT, BOTTOM   . . . the players lounge off the locker room, wall-to-wall comfort.

His language included the full range of rich rambling non sequiturs that came to be known as "Stengelese," both in the dugout, in his family's Valley National Bank of Glendale, and even in the halls of Congress, where he testified in 1958 before the Senate's Antitrust and Monopoly Subcommittee, as follows:

"I had many years that I was not so successful as a ballplayer, as it is a game of skill. And then I no doubt was discharged by baseball, in which I had to go back to the minor leagues as a manager and after being in the minor leagues as a manager I became a major league manager in several cities and was discharged, we call it 'discharged' because there is no question I had to leave."

When Senator Estes Kefauver, the subcommittee chairman, interrupted to bring the discussion back to the central point — a new law governing baseball's relations with its players — Stengel galloped ahead without breaking stride:

"Well, I would have to say at the present time I think baseball has advanced in this respect for the player help. That is an amazing statement for me to make, because you can retire with an annuity at fifty and what organization in America allows you to retire at fifty and receive money? I want to further state that I am not a ballplayer, that is, put into that pension fund committee. At my age, and I have been in baseball, well, I will say that I am possibly the oldest man in baseball. I would say that when they start an annuity for ballplayers to better their conditions, it should have been done and I think it has been done."

Kefauver then cleared his throat and steered the testimony to another witness, Mickey Mantle, asking if *he* had any observations on the desirability of applying the trust laws to baseball. To which Mantle replied, with total clarity: "My views are just about the same as Casey's."

By 1960, Casey's final year with the Yankees, his imprint was broadened to include a new member of the cast, a twenty-six-year-old outfielder from Fargo, North Dakota, named Roger Maris. He was a left-

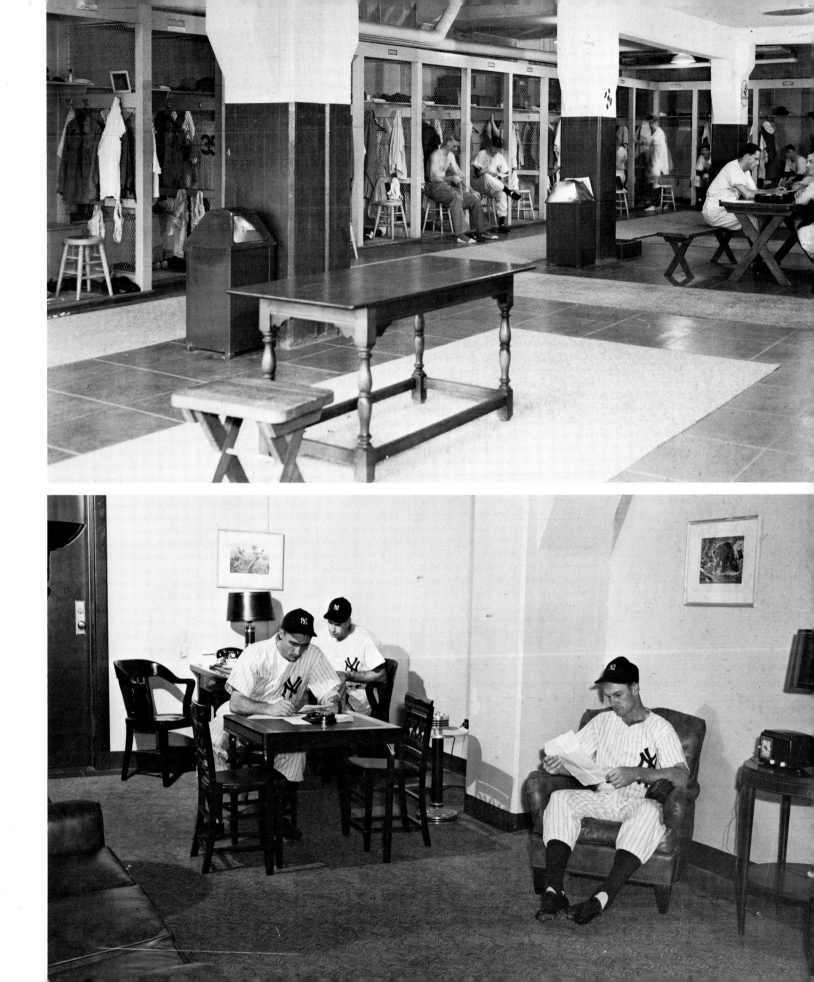

BELOW AND RIGHT   Command post: The scoreboard in right
field was modernized in 1959 with banks of electric switches
and a staff of "inside" communicators . . . translating into
lights outside the inning scores, who's at bat, the players'
positions, balls, strikes, hits, runs, and errors.

handed hitter with a severe crew cut and a severe, silent manner that prompted Stengel to perceive: "That Maris. You'd tell him something and he'd stare at you for a week before answering."

But Maris's saving grace was that during such a week, he might hit two or three home runs. And although he hit thirty-nine of them the first year the Yankees acquired him from Kansas City in a massive trade, he started to unload them in astonishing numbers the following season, 1961, after Ralph Houk had succeeded Stengel in the home dugout.

He didn't actually hit one until the Yankee's eleventh game, April 26 in Detroit, and after twenty games he had hit only three. But in four consecutive games in May, he drove four over fences and then took off on a home-run sweepstakes that twinned him for the rest of the summer with Mantle.

By June 1, he had hit twelve, putting him three days behind Ruth's pace of 1927, though that was still considered in a class with thinking about the unthinkable. On July 1, he hit number twenty-eight, and by now he was nine days (and five games) *ahead* of Ruth. By August 1, he had forty, which was six more than Ruth had hit thirty-four years earlier, and on September 1 he had fifty-one — which was eight more than the great man.

Now Maris, neck and neck with Mantle, stood where other sluggers had stood in the past without cracking any records — because in September 1927 Ruth bunched seventeen home runs together to reach his magic total

of sixty. But Maris tore down the homestretch as the crowds gathered, adding two on September 2 against Frank Lary and Hank Aguirre of Detroit and then three more by September 9 for a total of fifty-six.

By the one hundred fifty-fourth game of the season, on September 19, Maris had reached fifty-eight, still two shy of Ruth's 154-game bag. But two teams and eight games had been added to the schedule now, and in those eight remaining games Maris pumped three more home runs out of the lot — number fifty-nine off Milt Pappas in Baltimore, number sixty off Jack Fisher of the Orioles in Yankee Stadium, and the unthinkable number sixty-one off Tracy Stallard of Boston in the stadium on October 1.

Along the way, he had hit thirty at home and thirty-one on the road; forty-nine off right-handed pitchers and twenty off left-handers; thirty-six by day and twenty-five by night. Any way you sliced it — and people sliced it many ways, since many of them considered Maris a sort of intruder — he had hit more home runs in one major-league season than anybody else.

The irony of it was that Maris had trouble pleasing people who mourned either the passing of Ruth's record or the fact that it had been surpassed by a newcomer instead of by Mantle, who was injured that September and who finished with fifty-four. The Yankees also won 109 games that year, and won both the pennant and World Series, but in the closing stages of the race almost all the publicity and pressure were poured on Maris — a shy, uncommunicative man, obsessed with a desire for privacy, but a man who responded to his "ordeal" with good grace despite the tumult.

After every game down the stretch, his locker was besieged by crowds of newspaper writers and broadcasters who had latched onto the club to cover both races — the Yankees' and Maris's. They wanted to know what he had hit, what he had not hit, what he felt, what he thought, what he ate and drank, and, a few thousand times, whether he believed he'd break

LEFT AND BELOW   How to paint a foul pole . . . with the aid
of a boom crane in the annual housecleaning, a sort of
$400,000 face lift.

A great stadium by day . . .

. . . and by night . . .

... and sometimes you weren't even sure.

Ruth's record and, if so, how that would weigh on his conscience.

"Look," he would say, "Babe Ruth was a great ballplayer. Nothing I do can change that. But you can bet that I'll try to hit as many home runs as I can."

Another time, an out-of-town writer hot on the trail of personality trivia, asked if he had any interest in music. Maris replied that he liked popular music. Did he have a favorite singer? No, he guessed not. Well, would it be all right if the interviewer wrote that his favorite was Doris Day?

"How can you write Doris Day," asked Maris, incredulous by now, "when I say I don't really have a favorite?"

By then, his blond hair had begun to fall out, he hit another home run in the third game of the World Series, the Yankees knocked off the Cincinnati Reds in five, Maris was voted the most valuable player in the league for the second year in a row, and finally he headed home to Independence, Missouri — rich, famous, lionized, and somewhat puzzled by what he had wrought in that turbulent season of 1961.

December 28, 1958: For two years now, the New York football Giants have been sharing Yankee Stadium with the baseball Yankees, after thirty-one seasons in the Polo Grounds — where they were launched in 1925 for a $500 franchise fee by a legal bookmaker named Tim Mara. They went eight years without winning even an Eastern divisional title in the National Football League, then won three in a row starting in 1933, adding the league championship in 1934 with a 30 to 13 victory over the Chicago Bears in the storied "sneaker game." Four years later, in football shoes instead of sneakers, they won another division title and championship, and the divisional title the next year and twice during World War II.

Then came ten barren seasons until 1956, when they moved into the stadium, bulldozed the Bears again, 47 to 7, and began a run of five Eastern titles in seven years. Now Steve Owen has retired after twenty-three

Sometimes, when the ball club was on the road, the place would be taken over by circus acrobats . . .

years as coach, without a written contract, and Jim Lee Howell has held the reins for four. On this day, 64,185 persons are huddled in the seats; a winner's share is worth $4718, a loser's share $3111; the collective prize, the championship of pro football. The party of the second part is the Baltimore Colts, and later people would call it the greatest football game ever played.

The Baltimore quarterback is John Unitas, slightly stooped, slightly wolf-faced, slightly spectacular. Unitas knows that the Giants got that far by a well-knit, hostile defense that hounded other quarterbacks all season and came up with the ball often enough for New York's quarterback to operate — Charley Conerly, thirty-seven years old, matching chess moves with Unitas for a whole season's work.

Jim Parker, a second-year tackle, protects Unitas on defense from charging linemen like Andy Robustelli, and Unitas further turns the Giants' aggressiveness against them by picking, probing, changing signals at the line, sending his runners up the middle, hitting Lenny Moore with a long, flat sideline pass to New York's forty, and Moore carries it to the twenty-five for the first threat of the first quarter.

But the Giants defense holds and then performs above and beyond the call of duty by blocking the field-goal attempt. And then Conerly strikes back fast. With Baltimore's linebackers blitzing, he pitches underhand to Frank Gifford, who sprints thirty-eight yards to the Colts' thirty-one. Three plays later, Baltimore holds and Pat Summerall kicks a thirty-six-yard field goal, putting New York three points up.

In the second period, though, the pressure forces a break — against the Giants — when they fumble on their own twenty and the ball is smothered by Big Daddy Lipscomb, the 288-pound tackle. Now it's Unitas's turn to be relentless. He stays on the ground, feeding Alan Ameche and Moore, sending Moore to the outside once when the Giants bunch inside and then sending Ameche into the end zone from the two, putting Baltimore four points up after the conversion.

Next, Unitas starts on his own fourteen and begins to grind it out, like Rommel in the desert. His backs make five or six yards on repeated thrusts, then he connects twice with Raymond Berry, the second time for fifteen yards and touchdown number two. So, at half time, the Colts are in command with points to spare, 14 to 3.

Late in the third quarter, they are almost in command beyond belief after they rumble to New York's three-yard line with Unitas pinpointing his passes against the secondary, behind superb blocking. And now they stand four plays and three yards from stretching the lead to eighteen points — but just as suddenly, Howell's defense coalesces, with the immovable, back-to-the-wall stance that got the team into the title game in the first place. They deny Unitas' backs those last three yards, then turn upfield with a vengeance.

Conerly sends Kyle Rote far deeper than usual, far down the left sideline and then across to his right, where the pass is spinning across his path at the Baltimore forty. Rote stays in stride to the twenty-five, then gets crushed in a two-man scissors and the ball squirts loose. But Alex Webster — who later will become the coach of the team as it turns into the nineteen seventies — grabs it and barrels to the one. Mel Triplett hurdles the huge white line, Summerall adds the point, and now it's 14 to 10 instead of 21 to 3.

Second play of the fourth quarter: Conerly, who has been pitching to Rote and Gifford, switches to Bob Schnelker, his end, seventeen yards and then forty-six more. First down on the Baltimore fifteen. Conerly to Gifford on the five, Gifford ramming into the end zone. New York somehow leading, 17 to 14, and the Colts in late trouble.

Two minutes to go, and the Giants punt deep to the Colt fourteen, giving Unitas less than 120 seconds to go eighty-six yards or finish second best in the National Football League. But Unitas is inhuman, too. Three times he finds Berry's grasping hands in a stunning

And once each summer, the Jehovah's Witnesses drew
thousands to the ball park for their meeting . . .

drive from deep in the hole, and three times Berry makes maddening catches — the last time for twenty-two yards on New York's thirteen. And now, with seven seconds left on the clock, Steve Myhra swings his foot at the ball on the twenty and it tumbles over the crossbar for a 17 to 17 tie.

They will decide it now in overtime, after resting three minutes and tossing a coin to see who kicks off, winner take all. The Giants win the toss, the Giants receive. But they make no headway with the ball, punt to the Colts' twenty, and dare Unitas to do his damndest. And Unitas does.

Mixing passes with running plays, he calls an irresistible sequence of plays that moves Baltimore downfield. Ameche, the burly back from Wisconsin, hides on a trap and then storms through the overcharging line for twenty-three yards to the New York twenty. Berry curls into the backfield, eludes the defensive backs, and makes another great catch on the eight. Three plays later, Ameche puts his head down, wrapping the ball in both arms like a bear, and rumbles through the monsters hand-fighting one another across the obliterated line of scrimmage and doesn't stop until he is stomping what is left of the grass beyond the goal line.

The final score is 23 to 17, and the Giants later will win and lose championship games by fewer points than that, in the cold, in the rain, in the snow. But the game they will remember the longest is this one, and the enemies they will remember longest are Unitas and his favorite target, Raymond Berry. On this day in this stadium, Berry has caught twelve of Unitas's passes for 178 yards. He cannot run very fast, he has a bad back and bad eyes, he wears thick glasses off the field and contact lenses on the field, one leg is shorter than the other, forcing him to wear mud cleats on that shoe to equalize the difference. He is thin and looks undernourished and he is clearly whipped by fatigue. But the Giants do not begrudge Raymond Berry his moment when he blinks through his weak eyes after the brutality has subsided and says, with feeling: "It's the greatest thing that ever happened."

. . . and thousands came to hear the Reverend Billy Graham

Michael Burke rode the elevator to the private dining room in the CBS Building on the Avenue of the Americas, shook hands with Frank Stanton, the president of the company, and William Paley, the chairman of the board, and then knuckled down to lunch — and later to the investment portfolio that CBS had entrusted to him. They were sitting around over coffee when Burke leaned back in his chair and popped the question:

"How about the New York Yankees?"

It was the same question that John McGraw had popped to Colonels Ruppert and Huston nearly half a century before. And the answer this time cost CBS fourteen million dollars and a lot of headaches. It was 1964, and the Yankees were still clinging to the pinnacle — twenty-nine pennants and twenty world championships in forty-five years. But they all realized that a piece of the action in turbulent times could become an expensive proposition.

Still, like Ruppert and Huston and Barkis, they were willing. And, after the ball club had promptly tumbled from the peak a year later, they suddenly were the proud possessors of an empire under pressure. They came to grips with the situation by assigning Burke full-time to the Yankees, as president and chairman of the board, and two years later as he was making the transition, the telephone rang in his Manhattan apartment.

"It was from Bill Paley," Burke recalled. "He wanted to ask if I was really sure I knew what I was getting into, if I realized that I was leaving the security of CBS to run a subsidiary where I'd be on public view like a target, if I appreciated that I'd be vilified in the press when things didn't work. I told him I was sure, and he said okay."

In pursuit of his new career as a public target, Burke switched his base of operations from a midtown skyscraper to the ball park uptown. He was a tall and athletic man with credentials out of Ernest Hemingway, with whom he once had played football outside a saloon in wartime Paris. He had been a halfback at the University of Pennsylvania, a navy officer in World War II, a special agent who parachuted behind the German

The precise geometry of the baseball diamond provides a dramatic setting for an altar erected at second base, where Cardinal Spellman celebrates mass.

LEFT October 4, 1965: On the first visit by a Pope to North America, Paul VI is accompanied by Cardinal Spellman as he rides across the stadium turf . . .

lines on long-odds missions, a circus director, Hollywood scriptwriter, and television executive. Now he had a job that demanded some of the derring-do of all the previous ones: running a highly successful baseball team on the down side of the cycle in a clamorous generation against all sorts of rivals for what people called "the entertainment dollar."

"In my view," he reflected, "the goal of giving New York the finest in baseball has sociological ramifications at a time when people are increasingly surrounded by steel and pavements and are in need of the relaxation baseball brings."

Part of Burke's problem was to see that the people who paid their way into Yankee Stadium were surrounded by more than just steel and pavements — especially at a time when human values in general seemed to be under attack and when the Yankees in particular were being forced to retreat.

The ball club, in the midsixties, began to subside through a combination of strains both inside and out.

For one thing, the other teams in baseball had decided to distribute the talent by legislation through the "free-agent draft," an orderly selection of amateur players something like the draft in pro football. That is, the last shall be first and the first last, and in 1966, the Yankees duly became last in the American League. For another thing, though, the club's farm system could not reinforce a cast that kept losing its key members — Bobby Richardson and Tony Kubek retired from the game before turning into their thirties, Mickey Mantle struggled along on the two worst knees in the business until he retired in 1969, and Roger Maris, Clete Boyer, Tom Tresh, and Joe Pepitone all were traded in a hostile market.

That left the Yankees with an urgent need to rebuild or to wither, especially after the emergence of the Mets into the National League in the city's modern new Shea Stadium in Queens. It also left them with the football Giants as a restless tenant, unhappy with the shared space and seeking greener fields eventually across the

135

... and presides at mass before 80,000 persons, with personal visits from schoolchildren ...

Hudson River in New Jersey. The city, in 1972, offered to buy and refurbish the stadium, and the Yankees decided to stay in the splendor of new surroundings. But the task of rebuilding the image and of recapturing the memories remained.

The chief memories, as the ball park reached the fifty-year mark, were these:

Twenty-seven World Series had been played in it, twenty of them won by the Yankees. Twenty-nine boxing titles had been decided there, and three pro football championships. Political assemblies had been staged, evangelists had preached, acrobats had whirled, and "first balls" had been pitched by dozens of celebrities. It had been the forum for the Jehovah's Witnesses and the Billy Graham Crusade, and it had even been transformed into an outdoor church for masses presided over by Cardinal Spellman and Pope Paul VI.

Lights had been installed in 1946, putting the Yankees and Detroit Tigers and the Grambling football team under 2,400,000 watts; a $120,000 scoreboard in 1950; another in 1959, measuring 113 feet wide, 45 feet high, and $300,000 heavy; and a telephonic Hall of Fame in 1967 that supplied the voices of the men behind all those memories.

Sometimes stage props and lights were added for special events and they in turn added to the memories — unhappy ones, in the case of Sugar Ray Robinson on the night of June 25, 1952. A sweltering night in New York, and more sweltering under the ring lights in the stadium, where Robinson was trying to add another championship to a remarkable career that already included the welterweight and middleweight titles.

This time, the old smoothie of boxing was after the light-heavyweight crown held by Joey Maxim and, if Sugar Ray could do it, he would match the feat of Henry Armstrong a dozen years earlier — world titles in three divisions. For eleven of the fifteen rounds, it was no contest as Robinson danced and punched in that graceful, relentless style. But the temperature under those ring lights rose to 104 degrees and at the end of the tenth round, a casualty: Ruby Goldstein, the

... and with blessings from a prince of the church.

Faces in the crowd: Jim Farley, the man in the summer straw.

RIGHT   How about that?

referee, wilted in the heat and gave way to a relief referee, Ray Miller.

Then Sugar Ray began to wilt and, at the end of the thirteenth, he stumbled to a neutral corner. They finally hoisted him over to the stool in his own corner but could not revive him and, decisively ahead on points, he failed to answer the bell for number fourteen — a victim of "heat stroke," the first and only knockout of a career of otherwise illustrious memories.

In center field, 450 feet from home plate, three monuments added to the reminders of Babe Ruth, Miller Huggins, and Lou Gehrig. And behind them on the outfield wall, plaques to Ed Barrow and Jacob Ruppert and another to commemorate the papal mass of October 4, 1965.

The first night baseball game was played on May 28, 1946, with the Yankees losing to the Washington Senators, 2 to 1. Seven years later, the stadium and its grounds were sold to Earl and Arnold Johnson of Kansas City, who two years after that sold both to John William Cox, a Chicago banker. The price was six and a half million dollars, and it included the stadium of the Kansas City Blues, then one of the Yankees' farm clubs. The Yankee Stadium grounds then were sold to the Knights of Columbus for two and a half million dollars and, in 1962, Cox made a gift of the park itself to Rice University in Houston, Texas.

The playing field of three and a half acres and the complex of eleven and a half acres all got a face lifting in 1967, a $1,350,000 modernization job that included ninety tons of paint over 3,700,000 square feet of surface (twice).

Five parking lots outside the park were operated by the stadium with space for 1500 cars, which was one of the problems despite all the statistics and despite the fact that 3500 more cars could be parked within a few blocks. There were 190 telephones inside, 130 of which were used by the ball club, and a full-time ground crew of seventeen kept the grass cut — to a height of one and a half inches — every other day, while the pitching

Photographers, too. Alongside announcers, writers, and the television crews, the scene is captured by master lensmen like Ernie Sisto of the *New York Times,* who snapped them all from Babe Ruth to Bobby Murcer.

mound was surveyed and kept to a height of fifteen inches above home plate.

To water the field, the Yankees drew on their own well, and when it rained it took twenty-five men to roll up the canvas infield covering, an operation that once was timed in forty-eight seconds. But to clean the stands after a game, it took eight to ten hours, and to resod the field in the spring, five weeks.

To keep the field full for Fran Tarkenton and Mel Stottlemyre across the seasons, these supplies were needed:

> 120,000 square feet of sod
> 20 tons (400,000 pounds) of soil conditioner
> 8 tons of fertilizer
> 200 yards of topsoil
> 600 pounds of Merion Blue grass seed
> 2 tons of lime for marking
> 30 yards of brick dust for the track
> 10 yards of clay for pitcher's mound

Then, to handle the crowds from start to finish, it normally took an army of stadium helpers behind scenes that had been set for second basemen, goalies, and linebackers:

	Baseball	Football	Special Events
Ushers	100 — 350	325 — 350	150 — 600
Ticket takers	50 — 90	90 — 90	70 — 90
Special police	45 — 100	80 — 100	100 — 300
Ticket sellers	20 — 35	5 — 10	35 — 50
Management aides	8 — 15	15 — 15	15 — 30
Ground crew	30 — 30	30 — 35	30 — 40
Matrons	15 — 35	25 — 35	25 — 35
Sweepers	50 — 120	100 — 120	100 — 125
Electricians	2 — 4	3 — 4	10 — 15
Plumbers	2 — 3	2 — 3	2 — 3
Painters	1 — 1	1 — 1	1 — 5
Medical	2 — 12	2 — 12	2 — 12
Concessions	300 — 565	400 — 565	300 — 565
Total:	625—1360	1078—1340	840—1870

In addition, the Stadium Club operated bars and dining rooms upstairs and down, a television studio was

But whatever it is, a stadium is a place where people
gather — and scramble for foul balls . . .

. . . and while some may duck, some of the girls give it the old college try . . .

situated alongside the home clubhouse beneath the stands, a fifty-foot tower in center field brought public-address announcements through seventy-five speakers, and life-size portraits of old heroes kept the memories alive in the main lobby.

For some nonsporting special events, the logistics problems might have tested an army. The principal "outside" event, because of its size and frequency, was the convention of the Jehovah's Witnesses, which started in 1950 with an eight-day run and a peak attendance of 123,707 — far more than had ever made it for any World Series, football game, or other match. Far more than ever *could* make it, in fact, since the delegates not only filled all 70,000 or so regular seats but also filled 22,000 folding chairs set up around the ball field, with more than 25,000 other persons standing.

They were huge crowds, and in 1958 when the Polo Grounds held a simultaneous meeting, the Witnesses counted a total throng in both stadiums of 253,000 with 6000 volunteers acting as guides and patrol officers to keep order. And order was kept so carefully that the New York press marveled at what it called "well-disciplined" masses of people overflowing the ball parks for more than a solid week.

That summer alone, it took two chartered ships from Europe, sixty-five chartered planes from around the world, and streams of cars from around the hemisphere to channel the pilgrims into town — 4822 from Europe, 106 from Asia, 263 from Africa, 898 from Central and South America, 1341 from various islands, 17,000 from Canada, and more than 107,000 from the United States. They came from 123 countries, and they were joined by thousands more who created an immense trailer camp across the Hudson in New Jersey.

If the Yankees were playing on Sunday afternoon and the assembly was starting at 9 o'clock Monday morning, as often happened, the stage-setting began almost as soon as the third out in the ninth inning of the ball game. As many as thirty-five trucks loaded

145

Baseball is also little girls in big caps . . .

RIGHT   . . . and little boys in big caps . . .

LEFT ... and Thurman Munson's baby, no bigger than his mitt ...

... but basically, it's a small boy with a bat and a ball.

with equipment would converge on the stadium, unloading 65,000 pounds of tenting to be erected on the parking lots outside, with 950 stakes being driven into the ground to support the tents across three and a half acres.

The tents were assigned to French and Spanish delegates, who would listen to the program in their own languages, and also housed the cafeteria, dishwashing machines, and several refreshment stands. Under the tents alone, about 17,000 chairs were unloaded, along with 1200 plywood tabletops and 255 loudspeakers, including 70 inside the stadium itself. Then came the prefabricated stage, sixty by thirty feet, trucked in sections and assembled on the field near second base and marked by a watchtower of 30,000 artificial flowers.

The assemblies were convened in the stadium every two or three years to the wonderment of the regular Yankee staffs, who also marveled at the throng of 80,000 that filled the park on October 4, 1965, for the first visit to North America by a pope — Paul VI, who celebrated mass with Cardinal Spellman of New York and legions of bishops, monsignors, and priests. And again, apart from the significance of the event, the logistics were mountainous, even for the stadium people who wrestled with the arithmetic of crowds on all the other days.

Behind the mathematics, swarms of front-office deputies went at it twelve months of the year trying to replace the measurements with the magic that was needed to make any stadium a theater.

During the football season, the troupe was drilled by Tim Mara's son, Wellington, president of the Giants and father of ten children who ran pass patterns in a sweat suit for exercise some days. He was accompanied by people like his nephew, Timothy J. Mara II, next in command; Alex Webster, the one-time back who followed Owen, Howell, and Allie Sherman as coach; Don Smith, the director of public relations; and Dr. Anthony Pisani, an orthopedic surgeon whose patients ranged from Tucker Frederickson to Orlando Cepeda of the Atlanta baseball Braves.

149

BETTING PROHIBITED

And to the multitudes, baseball is the bleachers behind the great green stage.

For baseball, the ripples flowed directly from Burke to Lee MacPhail, the placid son of the tempestuous innovator Larry MacPhail and a general manager with a few notches in his belt dating to his days with the Baltimore Orioles. From CBS, an executive whirling dervish named Howard Berk handled more things than a utility infielder. Dr. Sidney Gaynor, another orthopedic surgeon, mended the muscles from Maris to Murcer. And, in a heavily trafficked office a few steps from the locker room, a vice president named Robert O. Fishel presided over public relations.

Fishel did not customarily resort to promotional sprees like those he had learned from Bill Veeck at Cleveland in the late forties or at St. Louis in the early fifties — for example, signing the midget Eddie Gaedel for one turn at bat with the Browns against the Detroit Tigers (Gaedel walked on four pitches from Bob Cain, who was broken up as much by laughing as by Eddie's telescoped strike zone). But regular visitors to the stadium often mourned the fact that Gaedel had not gone to bat in New York, where he might have been introduced by a public-address announcer named Bob Sheppard — the speech department chairman at John Adams High School and a man of impeccably cultured enunciation for both baseball and football.

For that matter, people would have given a lot to have seen Gaedel foisted on a manager like, say, Ralph Houk, who won three straight pennants starting in 1961 as the heir to Casey Stengel and who then returned to the dugout from the front office in 1966 when lean times set in. Houk, a one-time catcher and army major, was a cigar-smoking link to the good old days when making out a nine-man line-up was the most cheerful ceremony of the Yankee day.

An even longer link, though, was maintained in the clubhouse by Pete Sheehy, the equipment manager who came in from the cold — literally, one day in 1927 when they needed help inside and fished him out of the crowd at the gates. Since then, ten managers had come and gone through twenty-five World Series — but every winter, Sheehy relentlessly started packing 400 uni-

151

forms into twenty-five trunks for spring training. And he did it while also supervising the clubhouse for the football Giants, who took over as the Yankees left.

To Burke, all this was well and good because it kept the stadium going as a place of business, and the business was entertainment. But he was obsessed with the idea that baseball was fundamentally a one-on-one contest between a man pitching a ball and a man trying to hit it. So his problem, while restoring the ball club to the vicinity of its past prosperity, was to restore the romance of the ball club to the public.

It was a neat problem because the public's affections were usually lavished on folk heroes in sports, particularly folk heroes who did dramatic things. So while he set about the task of rebuilding the drama on the field, he began to festoon the stadium with the trappings of romance. He made a point of watching games from a box seat just off the home dugout, where he often signed more autographs than his ballplayers. He brought friends like Robert Merrill of the Metropolitan Opera to the stadium to sing the National Anthem. And, one day in 1968 while flying to Florida for spring training, he concluded that he was "personally bored with political figures on opening day," so he decided to ask Marianne Moore to heave out the first ball of the season.

His choice was remarkable because Miss Moore was not only a poet but an eighty-one-year-old poet at that. She had been born in St. Louis three years before Casey Stengel was born in Kansas City and, like Stengel, her credentials were flawless. She had seen it all from John McGraw to Yogi Berra; she had sculpted Mickey Mantle and Whitey Ford in verse and imagery; she once even kept a pet alligator named Elston Howard.

She was a tiny belle with braided white hair who lived until her death in 1972 in an apartment off lower Fifth Avenue, surrounded by clay and glass animals and by hundreds of books, and she did not keep Burke waiting long for a reply after he had dashed off a telegram to her.

"I am impetuous," she wrote back. "Can you imagine my delaying a moment upon receiving your telegram before writing you that I shall excitedly appear at Yankee Stadium on April 9th, even if I have not the best arm in baseball."

As things turned out, she didn't even wait until April 9, but instead startled the office staff by showing up at the side door of Yankee Stadium with her brother in March, while the club was still in Florida. "I wanted to see how far I had to throw it," she recalled later. "I thought I'd have to pitch it from the mound. I was

frightened by that. But they showed me the box seats where I was to sit, and gave me a ball and glove to take home."

She took the ball and glove home — "to practice," she said — and kept them in her bedroom as a reminder of the opening day she pitched a right-handed strike to Frank Fernandez, the young catcher, who returned it to her with a kiss on the cheek.

Fernandez also hit a home run that won the game, and somewhere between his act of gallantry to Marianne Moore and his act of devotion to the Yankees, the steel and concrete of the stadium made the magical transformation — to a stage, with people and the memory of people.

"Perhaps the single word 'tradition' is the clue," the *New York Times* said in an editorial once after the Brooklyn Dodgers had almost triumphed on that stage. "Perhaps when the chips are down, one pitches not to Mantle and Berra but really to Ruth and Gehrig. Perhaps in the clutch one faces not Reynolds or Raschi but really Gomez or Ruffing. Call it fighting spirit, inspiration or a muscular response to the memory of a crowd cheering long ago at a towering clout and a big man rounding the bases with bowed head and mincing step, doffing his cap to the stands.

"Call it what you will, the Yankees have it. The Dodgers' consolation is knowing that they did all and more than one can ask of mortal men fighting the ghosts of heroic deeds that compose what is commonly called 'tradition.' "

. . . and to all, a good night.

The Little Pigs'
PUPPET BOOK

by N. Cameron Watson

Little, Brown and Company

Boston Toronto London

Also by N. Cameron Watson
The Little Pigs' First Cookbook

First edition

Library of Congress Cataloging-in-Publication Data

Watson, N. Cameron (Nancy Cameron)
 The little pigs' puppet book / by N. Cameron Watson. — 1st ed.
  p.   cm.
 Summary: Three pig brothers decide to put on a puppet show for
all their friends. Includes step-by-step instructions for making
puppets, writing an original script, putting up a stage, creating
scenery, and making programs, tickets, and refreshments.
 ISBN 0-316-92468-7 (lib. bdg.)
 1. Puppets and puppet plays — Juvenile literature.   2. Puppet
making — Juvenile literature.   3. Puppet theaters — Juvenile
literature. 1. Puppet making.   2. Puppet plays. 3. Puppet
theaters.   4. Handicraft.] 1. Title.
PN1972.W38   1990
791.5'3 — dc19   89-30782
                                                         CIP
                                                          AC

10 9 8 7 6 5 4 3 2 1

WOR

Published simultaneously in Canada
by Little, Brown & Company (Canada) Limited

Printed in the United States of America

This book is dedicated to
Aldren Auld Watson
artist
teacher
father

Table of Contents

It is raining. The three brothers stare out the window.

"Bother!" says Charles.

"What a gloomy day," grunts Ralph.

"We could always read," remarks Bertram.

"I have a better idea," exclaims Charles. "Let's put on a puppet show!"

6

"First," says Bertram, "we have to make some puppets."
Each pig has a plan. Charles uses a sock for his
puppet. Bertram starts with a cardboard tube.
Ralph decides on a jaw puppet.

Sock Puppet

1. Find an old, clean sock (without holes!). Put your hand inside, with thumb in heel and fingers in toe. Pinch your thumb and fingers together. This will be your puppet's mouth.

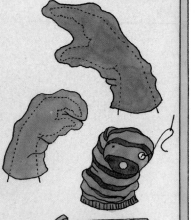

This puppet is very easy to make.

2. With puppet on, close its mouth. Use a marker to draw dots where the nose and eyes will go. Sew on buttons for eyes and nose.

3. Outline the mouth area with marker. Cut out an oval piece of fabric the same size as mouth area. Brush mouth area and wrong side of fabric with rubber cement. Let dry. Line up edges and press cemented side of fabric onto mouth area.

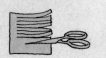

If you don't know how to sew, ask someone to help; or use rubber cement to attach eyes, nose, and hair.

Your mouth can be red, pink, or whatever color you'd like. Mine is blue!

If you sew well, you can sew the mouth on instead of cementing it.

4. Choose a fabric for hair. Cut out five 3″×3″ squares. Make fringe by cutting slits about ¼″ apart into one side of each square, leaving about ½″ at opposite side of square uncut.

Whenever you use rubber cement, protect your work surface with old newspapers.

5. Sew one fringed square onto puppet at top of forehead, with fringed end pointing away from puppet's face. Sew next square to puppet underneath first square, as shown, so that the first overlaps the second and the seams are ½″ apart. Repeat until all five squares are attached. Add more squares if necessary.

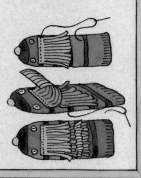

I always move the sock around and study it for a minute before marking the features. That way I get a better feeling for the character.

A. Thread needle and knot both ends of thread together.

B. Sew along fabric edge, using medium-long stitches.

C. Pull thread tight. Hold on to fabric so it bunches up against knot.

D. Fasten the gathers by sewing back and forth through them. Make a knot and cut off extra thread.

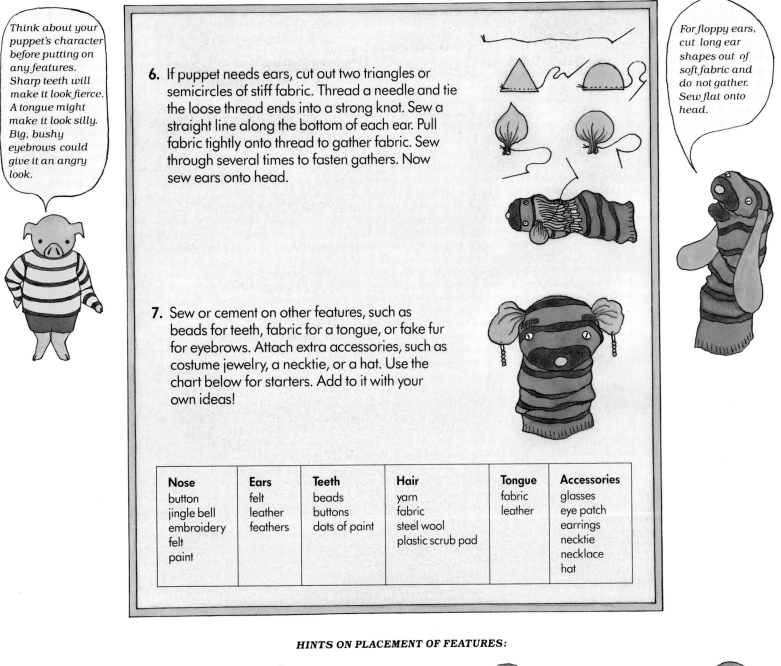

Think about your puppet's character before putting on any features. Sharp teeth will make it look fierce. A tongue might make it look silly. Big, bushy eyebrows could give it an angry look.

For floppy ears, cut long ear shapes out of soft fabric and do not gather. Sew flat onto head.

6. If puppet needs ears, cut out two triangles or semicircles of stiff fabric. Thread a needle and tie the loose thread ends into a strong knot. Sew a straight line along the bottom of each ear. Pull fabric tightly onto thread to gather fabric. Sew through several times to fasten gathers. Now sew ears onto head.

7. Sew or cement on other features, such as beads for teeth, fabric for a tongue, or fake fur for eyebrows. Attach extra accessories, such as costume jewelry, a necktie, or a hat. Use the chart below for starters. Add to it with your own ideas!

Nose	Ears	Teeth	Hair	Tongue	Accessories
button	felt	beads	yarn	fabric	glasses
jingle bell	leather	buttons	fabric	leather	eye patch
embroidery	feathers	dots of paint	steel wool		earrings
felt			plastic scrub pad		necktie
paint					necklace
					hat

HINTS ON PLACEMENT OF FEATURES:

eyes _far apart_

kindness, intelligence

eyes _close_

meanness, dullness

eyebrows _high_

surprise

eyebrows _low_

anger

9

Tube Puppet

You will need:
cardboard tube
ruler or tape measure
scissors
pencil
markers or
    poster paints
    and paintbrush
yarn
rubber cement
old newspapers
old, small sock
seam binding
fabric
needle and thread
felt or thin cardboard

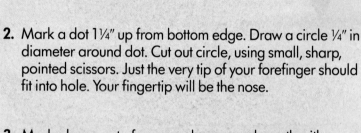

1. Find a cardboard tube 1½" in diameter. Cut off a 3"-long piece.

2. Mark a dot 1¼" up from bottom edge. Draw a circle ¼" in diameter around dot. Cut out circle, using small, sharp, pointed scissors. Just the very tip of your forefinger should fit into hole. Your fingertip will be the nose.

3. Mark placement of eyes, eyebrows, and mouth with a pencil. Draw features on with markers or poster paints.

4. Choose yarn for hair. Cut yarn into 2" lengths for short hair, 5" lengths for long hair. Brush hair area on puppet with rubber cement and let dry. Cement top 1" of hairs on one side and let dry. Press cemented hairs firmly onto head, one by one. Trim if necessary.

5. Cut 2" off the toe end of an old, small sock. This toe end will be the hat. Brush cement in a ½" strip along top edge of head and hair, and also in a ½" strip along the inside edge of hat. Let dry. Fit hat onto puppet's head and press edges of hat firmly onto cemented edge of head. To finish raw edges of hat, cut a 7" piece of seam binding and cement it over edge of hat, allowing ends of binding to overlap.

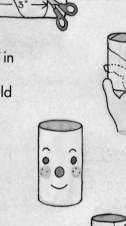

This puppet is a little more difficult to make.

You may want to ask an adult for help.

For simpler hair application:
Wind yarn loosely around your hand to make a "mop" of hair. Cement mop onto entire top edge of tube.

If sock is bigger than head, just gather edges a bit.

OTHER HAT IDEAS:

A. Cut a circle of fabric 4" in diameter. Gather and cement to edge of head. Finish with seam binding.

B. Sew a "sock hat" out of two pieces of fabric, as shown. Turn hat right-side out and attach to head as in step 5.

C. Look for a doll's hat that's the right size.

10

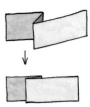

A pleat is a fold made by doubling material over on itself. You may want to practice making pleats in a piece of paper first; or ask an adult for help.

Choose a piece of fabric that suits your puppet's character.

Fold all the pleats down in the same direction.

Cut neat circles for arm holes. Use small, sharp, pointed scissors.

Always protect your work surface with old newspapers!

6. Cut out a rectangle of fabric for costume, about 8″ × 16″. Brush rubber cement in a ¼″ strip along the wrong side of one long edge of fabric. Let dry. Fold fabric into ¼″ pleats every ½″ along cemented edge, as shown.

7. Brush a ¼″ strip of cement along bottom edge of tube. Let dry. Press cemented edge of costume onto cemented edge of tube, starting and ending at back of puppet's head. Trim off excess fabric, leaving ½″ overlap. Cement the back opening shut.

If you sew well, you can sew the costume opening shut instead of cementing it.

8. Cement pleats down flat, using the same drying-and-pressing method.

9. Cut a 7″ piece of seam binding. Cement over raw neck edge of costume.

To make ears, cut out felt or thin cardboard semicircles. Attach flat edges to sides of head with rubber cement. Bend curved edges out slightly.

10. Try on puppet, putting forefinger into hole for nose. Mark on costume where the base of your thumb and the base of your pinky finger are. Take off puppet and cut ¾″ holes in costume for thumb and pinky. These fingers will be the puppet's arms.

TO MAKE A PIG'S SNOUT:

A. Cut nose hole big enough for first joint of forefinger to fit through.

B. Put an old thimble on finger. Mark pig's nostrils on end of thimble.

Jaw Puppet

You will need:
paper
marker
ruler
scissors
cardboard
fabric
straight pins
rubber cement
old newspapers
needle and thread
felt
buttons
yarn
book or pad
string

"To score" means to make a line with a sharp instrument. A score line helps you bend the cardboard neatly.

Be careful not to go all the way through the cardboard when you score it!

Cover your work surface with old newspapers so you don't get cement on it.

1. Lay your hand flat on a piece of paper with fingers together and thumb out, as shown. Draw an arc around fingers, leaving at least ½" all around, starting at "V" of thumb joint and going around fingertips to opposite side of hand. This is your pattern. Draw a straight line across the base of the arc.

2. Cut pattern out of paper. Transfer to heavy cardboard by outlining pattern. Then flip pattern over, line up along straight edge, and outline it again so you have a long oval with a straight line where the two halves of the pattern meet.

3. Cut out cardboard outline. With point of scissors and a ruler, make a hinge by scoring along the straight line. Fold along hinge line to make top and bottom jaws.

4. Choose a piece of fabric that is double the width of the jaw plus 6", and 14" longer than the length of the jaw. Fold fabric in half lengthwise and lay it down flat. Lay closed jaw on fabric with rounded tip of jaw 1½" from top edge and with each side edge of jaw 1½" from nearest side edge of fabric. Outline rounded edge of jaw on fabric, leaving 1½" all around, as shown. Cut along line through both layers of fabric.

This puppet is a bit complicated; you may need an adult's help.

These instructions are for the smallest size; you can make the jaw longer or wider if you'd like.

Pin together folded fabric if it won't lie flat while you cut it.

In choosing a fabric, think about color. A brown wolf might look nice, but a bright green one might look even nicer!

Also think about texture and thickness. Fake fur, velvet, and corduroy are nice for furry animals. But if the fabric is too thick, you won't be able to pleat it.

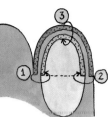

A. *Start at sides of jaw (1 & 2), then go to tip of jaw (3).*

B. *Go on to points halfway between attached points (4 & 5).*

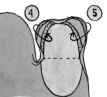

C. *Continue attaching at halfway points until entire fabric edge is attached.*

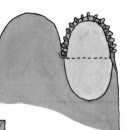

Close-up of pleats

A sewn seam looks much neater than a cemented seam.

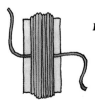

5. Open fabric flat, with wrong side up. Lay open jaw in place on fabric. Brush a ¼″-wide strip of rubber cement all around edge of jaw and rounded edges of fabric, as shown by shaded areas. Let cement dry.

6. Wrap cemented edge of one rounded section of fabric around cemented edge of one side of jaw, overlapping ¼″. Fold or pleat where necessary. Cement pleats down flat, using the same drying-and-pressing method.

7. Fold fabric lengthwise so that wrong sides are facing. Fold jaw along hinge line so that remaining jaw edge meets remaining cemented edge of fabric. Wrap fabric edge around edge of jaw and attach it as in step 6.

8. Sew shut the open side of puppet's body; or cement edges, let dry, and press together firmly.

9. To make ears, cut out two triangles or semicircles of stiff fabric. Thread needle and tie the loose thread ends into a strong knot. Sew a straight line along the bottom of each ear. Pull fabric tightly onto thread to gather fabric. Sew through several times to fasten gathers. (See page 9 for hints on gathering fabric.)

10. Sew on ears. Mark location and sew on button eyes and nose. Add tail, whiskers, tongue, or other extras if you like.

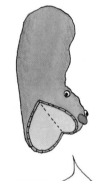

To cover pleats, cut a piece of felt the same size as inside of mouth and cement it to inside of mouth.

TO MAKE A TAIL:

A. *Wind a lot of yarn around a large book or pad. Slip a piece of string between book and wound yarn.*

B. *Tie string tightly in a knot to mark the top of the tail. Remove book.*

C. *Holding tail by string, wind another string around top of tail ½″ below first knot and tie tightly. Cut through loops at bottom of tail; trim.*

Or: *Cut out a tail-shaped piece of fake fur.*

13

When the puppets are finished, the pigs confer
on story ideas. Charles wants to make up a story
as they go along. Bertram would prefer using a
fairy tale.

14

The brothers finally agree on an original plot.
Ralph writes a script on his computer.

Script

While you make your puppet, start to decide on and practice a voice for it.

If you finish first, keep practicing until everyone else is finished.

I am a very rich and handsome wolf. I only like to eat butterscotch cream pie. I like to fly to Paris every weekend.

The puppet can be a person, an animal, an outer-space creature, or whatever you want.

1. Get together with three or four friends.

2. Make whichever puppet you want while your friends do the same.

3. With your finished puppets, sit in separate corners of the room. Experiment with various voices until you each have the perfect voice for your puppet. Practice your puppet's voice until it sounds really convincing.

4. Sit together in a circle with the puppets. Close your eyes, and imagine as hard as you can that you are your puppet. Open your eyes. Remember: you are now your puppet! Go around the circle and have each puppet introduce itself in turn, using its own voice. Each puppet should describe itself: personality, profession, hobbies, tastes in food and clothing, family background, and so on.

5. Now the puppets should talk together to see how they get along. Who likes whom? Which ones just can't seem to keep out of an argument?

6. Think of a problem that might come up between the characters. How did the problem arise? How does it make each puppet feel? What can they do to resolve the problem? The answers make a story. Write it down if you need to.

You can write down the lines and memorize them, but it takes a lot of time!

OR, IF YOU PREFER:

A. Choose a short fairy tale or folktale that you all know. The number of characters should equal the number of puppeteers.

B. Decide who will take which part. This is called casting. If you can't agree, draw straws or pick names out of a hat.

C. Each puppeteer should make the puppet for the part he or she has chosen. Have the puppets introduce themselves to each other as described above.

Rehearsal

Discuss the story together to decide how to divide it up.

Rehearsing can be hard work, but it will pay off in the final performance.

1. Divide the story into three parts: the beginning (setting the scene), the middle (introducing and developing the problem), and the end (resolving the problem). See the chart below for examples.

2. Act out the beginning part with the puppets, using their own voices. They should speak only to each other, not to the puppeteers. Work on the beginning until everyone is satisfied, then go on to the middle and end parts.

3. Ask a parent or friend for suggestions. Was the story clear? Could everything be heard? Was it funny enough? Was it serious enough? Change some lines if necessary.

The puppets should act out the story, not just tell it.

4. Rehearse the final version at least three times. The play is now almost ready!

Feel free to change the story a little if you think of better ideas as you go along. Rehearse again with the changes.

STORY	SETTING THE SCENE	DEVELOPING THE PROBLEM	RESOLVING THE PROBLEM
The Three Little Pigs	The three pigs leave home to seek their fortunes.	Wolf keeps eating pigs one after another.	Oldest pig outwits wolf and gets rid of him.
Hänsel and Gretel	Wicked stepmother loses children in forest.	Children are lured into witch's house; witch prepares to eat them.	Children trick witch and push her into oven.
Goldilocks and the Three Bears	Three bears live peacefully and happily in the woods.	Goldilocks disrupts the household: eats food, messes up beds.	Bears frighten Goldilocks; she runs away and leaves them in peace.

The pigs begin to rehearse. Ralph gets grumpy
when Charles can't remember his lines. Charles
thinks Ralph is too bossy. But Bertram keeps them
going, and finally the play comes together nicely.

"How about building a stage?" says Ralph. Charles wants to set up a quick stage behind the table. Ralph suggests using a box. Bertram insists on making a stage to fit in the doorway. They all get to work.

19

 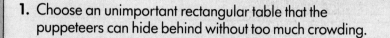 

Table Stage

rectangular table
old sheet or other
    large cloth
thumbtacks or
    masking tape
string
colored paper
fabric scraps
scissors
rubber cement
old newspapers
straight pins
odds and ends

If the table is not wooden, use strong tape instead of thumbtacks for all fastening.

If table has a lower support that gets in the way,

you can keep table in its upright position.

1. Choose an unimportant rectangular table that the puppeteers can hide behind without too much crowding.

2. Tip table over gently onto one long side. Set table in the spot chosen for the stage, with tabletop facing audience area.

3. Choose an old sheet, tablecloth, or other large piece of fabric for your stage cover. Drape fabric over tabletop so the bottom edge of cloth just touches the floor. If necessary, fasten in place with thumbtacks on *back* of tabletop.*

4. Pull sides of fabric around to make a neat edge on both sides of stage. Tie in place or fasten with thumbtacks on *inside* edge of table legs.*

5. Pin or cement decorations to fabric covering front of stage. Here are some decoration ideas:

colored paper	old buttons	cotton balls
fabric scraps	balloons	colored tape
feathers	streamers	beads
yarn	flowers	odds and ends

Ask your parents if you can use the table and sheet!

If the table seems tippy at all, place a heavy box or similar object against the front side so it can't tip over.

*Check first with parents!

Remember to put down newspapers if you use rubber cement.

For a winter scene:
A. *Choose a dark cloth.*
B. *Pin white cloth or paper onto it for snowy ground.*
C. *Glue on lots of cotton balls for snow.*

For a summer scene:
A. *Choose a sky-blue cloth.*
B. *Pin green fabric onto it for grassy ground.*
C. *Pin on a paper sun. Add paper birds, flowers, or trees.*

Box Stage

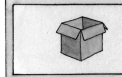
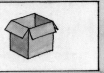

You will need:
large carton
marker
utility knife
scissors
poster paints
paintbrushes
old newspapers
fabric scraps
colored paper
rubber cement
stapler and staples

If you store the stage carefully in a safe place, you can reuse it many times.

1. Find a big, empty cardboard carton that is large enough for all the puppeteers to fit into. Decide whether you want the box upright or on its side. This will depend on how everyone fits best into the box.

2. Choose one side of the box to be the front. Mark where you want the stage opening to be. The hole should be high enough so that the puppeteers' bodies cannot be seen, but low enough to be within puppeteers' reach. The opening can be any shape, and you can have more than one opening if you want. Cut out opening with scissors or utility knife.

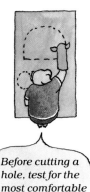

Before cutting a hole, test for the most comfortable height.

This makes a small stage, and works best for a play with only one, two, or three puppeteers.

Ask an adult for help with cutting the hole. A utility knife works best.

3. If necessary, cut out a low rear entrance door to stage. Leave at least one inch of cardboard on both sides of opening to keep the box strong.

Everyone should agree on the colors before you start decorating the stage.

4. To finish stage, paint with poster paints, or decorate with fabric or paper. Attach fabric and paper with rubber cement or staples. (See step 5 on page 20 for other ideas.)

If you use poster paints, cover the floor with old newspapers first.

TO MAKE A MINIATURE STAGE:

A. Find a carton large enough for just the puppets to fit into.

B. Cut out opening and decorate, following above directions.

C. Set up stage on a table to present the play.

Doorway Stage

You will need:

tape measure
12' of 1"×2" pine
crosscut saw
pencil
square
hammer
#6 finish nails
fabric
needle and thread
rubber cement
staple gun and ⅜"
    staples (or tacks)
heavy corrugated
    cardboard
utility knife
poster paints
paintbrushes
old newspapers

To square frame's corners:

A. Lay the square against a corner of the frame as shown.
B. Adjust corner of frame so it lines up with corner of the square.
C. Check the other corners of the frame in the same manner.

If you want a pleated curtain, cut it 14" wider and put a 1½" pleat under every staple or tack.

1. Measure the inside width of the doorway you have chosen for your stage. Subtract 1¾" from your measurement. This will be the length of your crosspieces.

2. On 1"×2" pine board, measure off two crosspiece lengths. Mark saw lines, using a square, and saw through to make crosspieces.* Then measure and cut two more pine sections, both 25" long, for side pieces.

3. Place the two crosspieces between the two 25" side pieces as shown and nail together the frame, using two #6 finish nails in each corner.

4. For the curtain, cut out a piece of fabric 45" long and 1" wider than the total width of the frame. Sew a ½" hem on all sides, or hem using rubber cement. Tack curtain to top surface of lower edge of frame, with right side of fabric facing up.

5. Lay frame on a flat piece of heavy corrugated cardboard. Square the corners of the frame. Outline outside edges of frame on cardboard. Cut out outline, using a utility knife.*

6. Mark stage opening on cardboard square, following measurements shown. Cut it out with utility knife.*

7. Matching edges evenly, tack cardboard to frame, with top edge of curtain pinned between cardboard and frame.

8. Decorate cardboard as desired, using poster paints. (Work on old newspapers!)

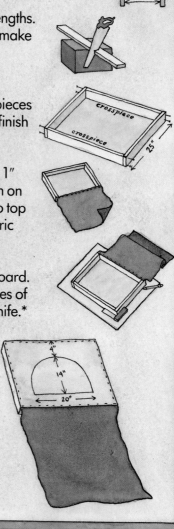

Measure doorway across the top and across the bottom and use the smaller measurement if they differ.

To cut wood:
A. Measure and mark.
B. Draw a pencil line across board with square.
C. Saw right next to line so line is left on measured piece.

*Ask an adult to help with sawing, nailing, stapling, and cutting with utility knife.

Put a scrap piece of wood or cardboard beneath your work while using a utility knife.

To tack curtain and cardboard:
Use a staple gun and ⅜" staples; or use long thumbtacks. Tack every 4".

A. Cut two wooden wedges 5" long, 2" wide, and ½" thick at the broad end.* (Or use strips of shingles for wedges.)

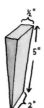

TO SET UP STAGE:

B. Hold stage at desired level in doorway. Tap wedges in between stage frame and doorjamb on top and bottom, as shown.

C. Check stage for proper height. Adjust if necessary. Put a footstool behind stage for very little pigs.

22

The stage looks beautiful. "Bertram was right,"
admits Ralph.

"A stage like that needs some proper scenery,"
says Charles. He gathers his materials and begins.

23

Scenery

You will need:
paper
pencil
old bed sheet
ruler or tape measure
scissors
4' × 8' plywood sheet
pushpins (or
    thumbtacks)
boxes or table
poster paints
tin cans or
    plastic cups
plastic spoons
paintbrushes
old newspapers
string
2 floor lamps
rubber cement

For Table Stage and Doorway Stage

1. Design your scene on a piece of practice paper.

2. Find an old, light-colored bed sheet. Cut off a 3' × 6' piece.

3. Lay sheet flat on an old piece of plywood. Tack sheet edges onto plywood with pushpins, starting at the corners of the sheet. Tack every 12". Stretch sheet tightly as you go.

4. Prop plywood against two boxes or an old table. Spread newspapers beneath plywood. Paint scene on sheet. Let dry.

5. Remove pushpins. Cut four pieces of string, each 12" long. Tightly tie a piece of string around each corner of sheet.

6. Place a sturdy floor lamp on each side of rear stage. Tie scenery onto posts, as shown. Leave a 12" space between front of stage and scenery so puppets have room to move.

For Box Stage

1. Design your scene on a practice piece of paper.

2. Cut out a piece of paper the same size as back side of box.

3. Paint scene on paper. Let dry.

4. Brush rubber cement on back side of scenery and on inside back of box. Let dry. Press cemented side of scenery to inside back of box.

Ask if you can have the sheet before you cut it!

Always protect your work surface with old newspapers.

Use old tin cans or plastic cups for paint holders. Use extra containers to mix colors in. Use plastic spoons for stirring paint.

Mix your own colors:

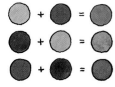

Use colors that aren't too bright, or else the scenery will overpower the puppets.

Make sure the objects in your scenery are large enough for the audience to see from a distance.

"Then we'll need music, programs, tickets, and, of course, some refreshments," pronounces Bertram. He makes up the programs and tickets while Charles retires backstage to set everything up. Ralph goes to the kitchen to prepare some special treats.

25

Special Effects

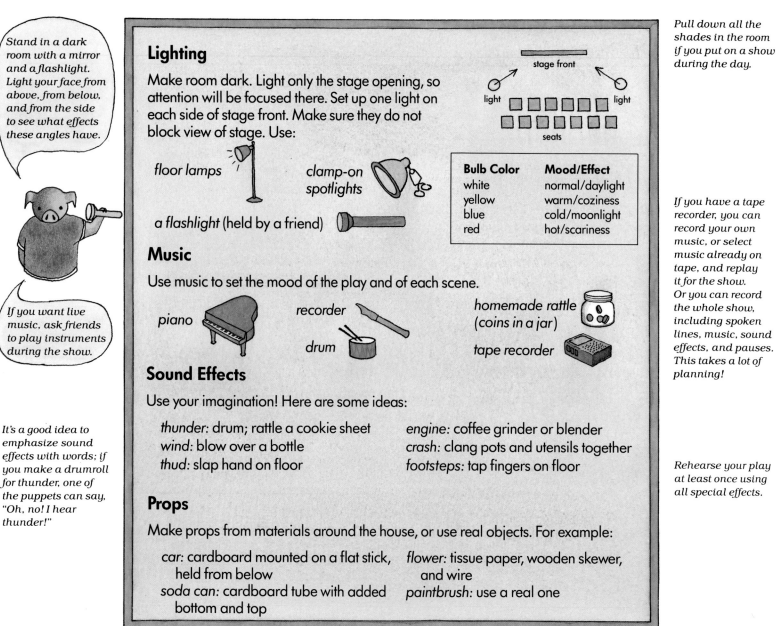

Pull down all the shades in the room if you put on a show during the day.

Stand in a dark room with a mirror and a flashlight. Light your face from above, from below, and from the side to see what effects these angles have.

If you want live music, ask friends to play instruments during the show.

Lighting

Make room dark. Light only the stage opening, so attention will be focused there. Set up one light on each side of stage front. Make sure they do not block view of stage. Use:

floor lamps

clamp-on spotlights

a flashlight (held by a friend)

stage front

light

light

seats

Bulb Color	Mood/Effect
white	normal/daylight
yellow	warm/coziness
blue	cold/moonlight
red	hot/scariness

If you have a tape recorder, you can record your own music, or select music already on tape, and replay it for the show. Or you can record the whole show, including spoken lines, music, sound effects, and pauses. This takes a lot of planning!

Music

Use music to set the mood of the play and of each scene.

piano

recorder

drum

homemade rattle (coins in a jar)

tape recorder

It's a good idea to emphasize sound effects with words; if you make a drumroll for thunder, one of the puppets can say, "Oh, no! I hear thunder!"

Sound Effects

Use your imagination! Here are some ideas:

thunder: drum; rattle a cookie sheet
wind: blow over a bottle
thud: slap hand on floor

engine: coffee grinder or blender
crash: clang pots and utensils together
footsteps: tap fingers on floor

Rehearse your play at least once using all special effects.

Props

Make props from materials around the house, or use real objects. For example:

car: cardboard mounted on a flat stick, held from below
soda can: cardboard tube with added bottom and top

flower: tissue paper, wooden skewer, and wire
paintbrush: use a real one

Cut holes for windows.

Cement or tape flat stick onto cardboard.

Tape cardboard circles onto bottom and top of small tube to make a soda can.

Bunch up tissue paper; wrap tightly around skewer with thin wire. Or use a real flower!

Programs and Tickets

You will need:
practice paper
pencil and eraser
ruler
scissors or
   utility knife
heavy paper or
   oak tag
markers or pen

Cut programs and tickets with sharp scissors; or, for crisper edges, ask an adult to cut them for you with a utility knife.

For clean lettering, use a fine-tipped artist's marker or a quill pen and india ink.

Use paper with a hard (smooth) finish so ink will not bleed.

Programs

1. On a piece of practice paper, write down the play's title and author(s). List the characters and their puppeteers. List where and when each scene takes place. List other credits: scenery, music, lighting, and so forth.

2. Look at your draft. The most important information should be in the largest letters. There should be a space between each section so everything can be read easily.

3. Cut another piece of practice paper to program size. Rewrite the program with the revisions. Does it look better? Is it easy to read? Make any necessary changes.

4. Cut your heavy paper to proper size. Carefully letter the programs with markers or pen. Decorate with borders or drawings if desired.

Tickets

1. On a piece of practice paper, write the play's title, the admission price, and the date of the performance. Try to fit all information into a 1½″ × 3″ space. Make the space a little larger if necessary. Write down measurements of space needed.

2. Cut tickets out of heavy paper, using the measurements from step 1. Carefully letter the tickets with markers or pen.

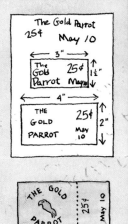

A program gives the viewer an idea of what the play is about, but it doesn't give away any secrets!

If you expect a large audience, you can write out one copy on white paper and photocopy the rest.

Tickets should be small so they can fit easily into a wallet or pocket. Keep them in a safe spot until you are ready to sell them!

LETTERING HINTS:

A. *Before lettering, use a ruler to draw very light pencil lines across the page showing where tops and bottoms of letters will go. These will keep words straight and letters uniform in height. Erase your guidelines neatly when finished.*

B. *Experiment with all capitals and with upper and lower case. Look in a type specimen book (check the library) for examples of different lettering styles.*

THE GOLD PARROT
The Gold Parrot
THE GOLD PARROT
The Gold Parrot

by Ralph
BY RALPH
by Ralph

27

Popcorn was first cultivated by American Indians.

Popcorn
(makes about 12 small servings)

1. Heat 1 tablespoon vegetable oil and 3 kernels popcorn in a large covered saucepan over high heat until kernels pop.

2. Add ½ cup kernels. Cover pan. When corn begins to pop, shake pan vigorously over heat until popping stops.

3. Pour immediately into large serving bowl.

You can add salt or melted butter, but plain popcorn is much better for you!

Fruit and Nut Mix
(makes 3 cups, or about 12 small servings)

Other nuts to use:
pecans
almonds
brazil nuts
hazelnuts

1. Mix: ½ *cup shelled walnuts*
   1 cup shelled peanuts
   1 cup raisins
   ½ cup dried apricots

2. Serve in large bowl or in small paper cups or packets.

Other fruits to use:
dried apples
dried pears
dried peaches
prunes

Prunes are dried plums. Raisins are dried grapes.

Fruit Punch
(makes about 12 small servings)

Other tasty combinations:
A. apple juice
   cranberry juice
B. pineapple juice
   cranberry juice
   squeeze of
      lime juice
C. grape juice
   raspberry juice
   squeeze of
      lemon juice

1. Blend in blender until very smooth:

   2 cups orange juice
   ¼ cup lemon juice
   1 large, very ripe banana,
      peeled and broken into chunks

2. Store in refrigerator until ready to serve. Reblend just before serving.

3. Serve in small paper cups. (The serving packets shown below will leak!)

If you don't have a blender, mash banana through a sieve and stir into the orange and lemon juice. Restir before serving.

TO MAKE PAPER SERVING PACKETS:

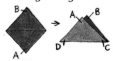

1. *Fold an 8"-square piece of paper in half diagonally.*

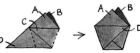

2. *Fold along dotted lines, as shown.*

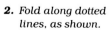

3. *Fold point A down and tuck into front pocket.*

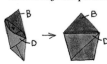

4. *Turn packet over and fold point B down flat, as shown.*

5. *To open, press top corners together gently.*

The show begins. Charles is nervous, but then he speaks his first line, and the performance is off to a promising start. The audience is enthralled.

After the show, everyone stays for refreshments.
Charles's wonderful puppet is passed around.
Bertram's fine design and lettering on the
programs are admired.

Several older pigs approach Ralph and give the
budding young author their congratulations. The
evening has been a great success.

Outside it is dark, and the sky is clearing.
Tomorrow will be a fine, sunny day. But the
brothers are eagerly awaiting the next rainy
day and what it might bring.